BENGALI
Myths

THE • LEGENDARY • PAST

BENGALI
Myths

T. RICHARD BLURTON

THE BRITISH MUSEUM PRESS

This book is dedicated to the memory of my father Thomas Richard Blurton and is for my mother Barbara Evelyn Blurton.

Acknowledgements

For fruitful discussions during the preparation of this book, I acknowledge with gratitude the following: Frances Carey, Biswajit Chakraborty, Sagar Chaudhury, Rosemary Crill, Anna Dallapiccola, Sona Datta, Rebecca Dobbs, Brian Durrans, Krishna Dutta, Jeremy Jeffs, Anne Kershen, George Michell, Sheila O'Connell, Pratapaditya Pal, Ruby Palchoudhuri, Venetia Porter, Urmi Rahman, Andrew Robinson, Tony Stewart, Jane Emerson Thors, John Williams and Michael Wood.

At British Museum Press, it is a pleasure to record the names of Isabel Andrews, Teresa Francis, Rosemary Bradley and especially my editor Colin Grant.

Finally, I owe special thanks to Martin Williams.

© 2006 The Trustees of The British Museum

T. Richard Blurton has asserted his right to be identified as the author of this work.

Published by The British Museum Press
A division of The British Museum Company Ltd
38 Russell Square, London WC1B 3QQ
www.britishmuseum.co.uk

A catalogue record for this book is available from the British Library.

ISBN-13: 978-0-7141-2436-0
ISBN-10: 0-7141-2436-2

Designed and typeset in Sabon by Janet James
Cover design by Jim Stanton
Printed and bound in Italy by Printer Trento Srl

FRONT COVER: *Register from a storytelling scroll-painting depicting the Muslim saint Gazi riding on a tiger (see p. 68).*

FRONTISPIECE: *The goddess Durga is venerated in Bengal during Durga Puja each autumn. Here, in the private shrine of the Pratap Chandra Chanda family in north Calcutta, priests honour the temporary image of the goddess made for the Puja, providing her with light, incense and flowers. October 2005.*

OPPOSITE: *The final register in a storytelling scroll-painting of the* Ramayana *showing Rama and Sita enthroned (detail; see p. 73).*

Contents

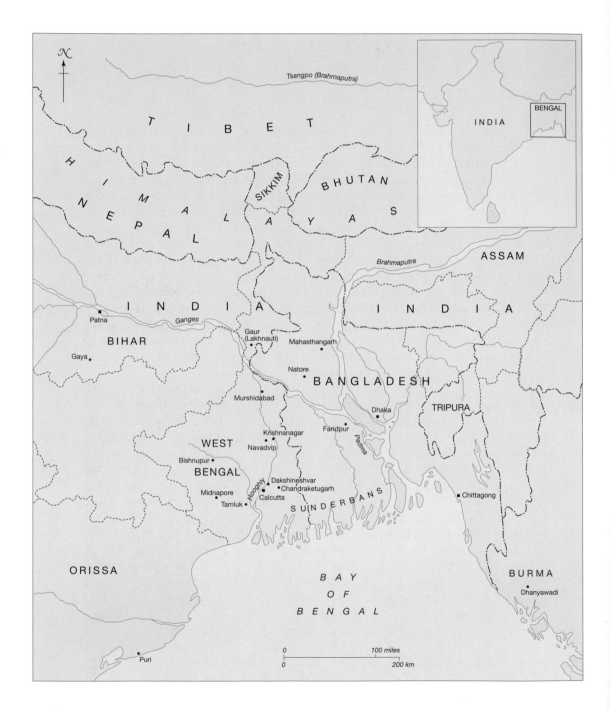

Introduction

This book presents narratives, especially those of myth and legend, from Bengal in the eastern part of South Asia. They are illustrated with paintings, sculpture and other objects from the collections of the British Museum. The myths have been chosen not only because they provide an opportunity to reproduce the Museum's magnificent range of objects from Bengal but also because they encapsulate much that is important about the culture of that region. They prompt discussion about the position of oral transmission and storytelling, the development of regional variants of pan-Indian myths, and the myth-making around the Muslim saints Gazi and Manik, both of whom inhabit that intriguing zone where Hindu and Muslim narratives intermingle. These stories, even those that are part of larger pan-Indian tales such as the myth of Krishna, exhibit features that are specific to Bengal and can thus be discussed here as ineluctably Bengali. Conversely, narratives known in Bengal but also throughout India and with no specific Bengali elements to them have been excluded. Further, in the story of the goddess Durga it is possible to show the extent to which worship of the goddess in Bengal has acted as an incentive to much other artistic activity in eastern India – poetry, music, sculpture, painting and, in modern times, journalism, radio and television.

Today, Bengal is divided into two parts, the sovereign country of Bangladesh and the state of West Bengal in the Union of India, but throughout most of their recorded history what are now two separate entities have functioned as a single cultural unit. This unity is most immediately evident in a common language written in a common script and known to the inhabitants as Bangla (rendered as Bengali in English). Many other features beyond language and script are also shared, such as diet, dress, musical traditions and literature, to name only a few. However, today there is a political bifurcation between these two areas based on religion, with the predominant faith of West Bengal being Hinduism and that of Bangladesh being Islam. Significant numbers of Hindus, though, are still resident in Bangladesh, just as many Muslims continue living in West Bengal. Given this situation, it is only to be expected that the culture of the region is complex. The myths represented here have been current throughout the entire area but are mostly concerned with the deities and cults of Hinduism, despite a certain amount of cross-over. Yet they are first and foremost Bengali stories, irrespective of which religion is dominant in the narrative.

The main exception to the Hindu preponderance in this book are the stories – still imperfectly understood – that concern the Muslim saints, or *pirs*, Gazi and Manik (pp. 67–72) and are illustrated in one of the finest works of art from the non-urban traditions of the Indian subcontinent preserved in the British Museum. This is a painted scroll over 13 metres (42 feet) in length and of the type used by itinerant storytellers. First published only fifteen years ago, it is still divulging its secrets.

The word 'myth' provides us with some interesting and perhaps controversial ideas. The idea of 'narrative' certainly seems to be embedded in 'myth' but whether veracity is there as well is more difficult to say. Also, what is the difference between 'myth', 'legend' and 'folk tale'? Whether all the narratives discussed in this book are all truly myths is uncertain; some readers may feel that 'legend' or 'folk tale' might be a better description for some or all of these stories. Nevertheless, mythical narrative is an intriguing though sometimes difficult subject. To start with, it is usually ahistorical and can be fixed in time only approximately; after all, the activities of the gods or of saints are by definition outside time. Secondly, the transmission of most myths – at least for the majority of their 'lives' – is connected to orality and to the performative presentation of stories, which is, obviously, difficult to replicate in a book.

Once myths become written down and even published, they move away from the impromptu fluidity of oral performance and become static, losing their vitality. It is for this reason that much of the material presented in this book is linked to performance, whether as part of a religious festival or as recitals given by itinerant storytellers or masked dancers. Even the viewing of cheaply produced but ephemeral printed imagery often had such a linkage, as this is frequently part of the drama of worship, of 'puja'. Almost all of the stories described here have a long 'prehistory' of oral transmission and performance, and in this respect they belong to one of the oldest and most substantial elements of South Asian culture. This is a culture that has, for millennia, mostly transmitted its lore through speaking, singing – and listening – rather than through writing.

The question of who the Bengalis are is complicated. Certainly their language represents – along with Assamese to the north – the most eastward extent of the large family of Indo-European languages, so some link with the population of the rest of northern India is apparent, though the connecting of ethnicity necessarily with language is an uncertain enterprise. Nevertheless, scholars suggest that by the middle of the first millennium BC groups of Indo-Aryan speakers had begun to penetrate into the eastern part of India, interacting and intermarrying with existing populations. These incomers must always have been comparatively few in number, despite the survival of their language system, a survival no doubt ensured by their use of new metallurgical and agricultural technologies.

It is also clear that elements from the immediate surroundings have contributed to the making of the Bengalis, and the proximity of groups who speak Tibeto-Burman languages (to the north and east), and even Mon-Khmer languages (also to the north), has left its mark on the racial make-up of this region. Throughout its history Bengal has witnessed many periods when incomers have settled and contributed to the racial mix. These include brahmin settlers in the early medieval period, mostly brought in from northern

India as religious specialists; Turkish, Afghan and Persian invaders in the late twelfth century, setting up their capital at Gaur in northern Bengal; further Muslim groups, who came with the establishment of Mughal power under Akbar in the sixteenth century; and finally a mixture of Europeans (Portuguese, Dutch, French and English) from the seventeenth to the twentieth centuries, who came first as traders and then – in the case of the British – stayed as rulers. Not surprisingly, given this variety of factors, a number of different religions have been practised in Bengal over the last two millennia – Buddhism, Jainism, Hinduism, Islam and Christianity – and have all had an effect on the myths of the region.

The question of religious affiliation in Bengal has, of course, deeply affected its culture. Two other contributory factors must also be briefly discussed before embarking on the narratives themselves: the geography and the history of the region.

The geography of eastern India

The story of Bengal and the rich oral literature it has produced are closely connected to the landscape of this eastern part of the Indian subcontinent. The dominant aspect of the land is flat, fruitful and riverine, although its edges – westwards towards the south Bihar plateau and eastwards towards the hills of Tripura and Chittagong – are drier, more broken and upland in character. In the central and northern part of Bengal two of the mightiest rivers of Asia, the Ganges and the Brahmaputra, meet and descend in conjunction into the Bay of Bengal to the south; both, however, rise far away to the north, in the Himalayas. The source of the Ganges is on the southern, Indian side of the mountains, but far to the west of Bengal, at Gangotri. Meanwhile, the Brahmaputra rises on the northern side of the Himalayas in Tibet, flows from west to east along the entire length of that country, where it is known as the Tsangpo, and only finally cuts through the mountain chain in the modern Indian state of Arunachal Pradesh. It then descends through Assam as the Brahmaputra and thus reaches Bengal, where in parts it is known as the Padma (see map, p. 6). Geologically, Bengal lies within the flood plain of these two massive river systems, and, depending on ice-melt in the far-off Himalayas and the intensity of the monsoon rains in the plains, the river brings rich fertilization to the fields of Bengal or disastrous flooding – or both. The joining of the two great rivers is shocking in its intensity. This intensity is compounded by the cyclones that are a recurring feature of the Bay of Bengal and sweep through the delta with destructive force. The river and its bounty act almost as a metaphor for much in the civilization of Bengal, for the utterly desirable can equally, and paradoxically, be immensely destructive. Not surprisingly, this element of the quixotic in the cosmos is reflected in the narratives generated or adapted in the delta landscape of Bengal.

As if this were not enough, the river valleys of the Ganges and the Brahmaputra mark the edge of two tectonic plates of the earth's surface. The dramatic meeting of these two plates, those of Eurasia to the north and of peninsular India to the south, has caused the uplift of the Himalayas. The

The source of the Ganges, Gangotri, in the Indian Himalayas as envisaged by a Bengali artist. The goddess of the river, Ganga, is depicted riding on her water-monster mount. Oil painting on canvas, Bengal, c.1890.

southern plate has pushed down below the northern plate, forcing the Eurasian plate upwards, thus forming the mountain chain in which are found the three highest mountains in the world. This process of uplift still continues (though partly countered by erosion) and is a source of seismic instability along the whole length of the Himalayas and throughout the valleys, such as those of the Ganges and the Brahmaputra, that lead out of them. Indeed, not only is this process of elevation still taking place but two other, though related, changes are in evidence. Firstly, the furthest edges of the delta of the combined Ganges–Brahmaputra, in Bengali known as the Sunderbans, is still extending out into the Bay of Bengal, slowly but inexorably, as a result of the vast quantity of silt that the rivers bring down with them from higher up the river valleys. These new lands are fertile and thus attractive for settlement, but also low lying and liable to flooding. Secondly, the waterways of the joined Ganges–Brahmaputra are slowly moving eastwards, with the result that the water systems of the delta are carving out new channels and abandoning others. This results in vast quantities of water becoming available in previously less watered regions, and the reverse in the abandoned areas. Also, settlements based on the old water channels to the sea are now silted up and losing their importance.

The history of the delta country is filled with stories of these vitalizing and also disastrous changes of the river systems. The great city of Calcutta, situated on a western waterway of the delta, the Hooghly, has always been subject to this uncontrollable move to the east of the fructifying, as well as scouring, waters of the Ganges. The city is increasingly unconnected to the delta of the massive river system and its waterways are silting up. This is but the latest and to us the most obvious of many shifts of river channels that can be traced from at least the first centuries AD. Similarly, the eastern delta has now for many centuries seen greater fluvial action, which has increased agricultural potential. This, it has been suggested, may explain why Islam spread so successfully in the eastern part of the delta compared to the western part. The arrival of Islam in Bengal in the second millennium AD coincided with the increasingly watered and fructified areas becoming available – and available to support newly converted populations. A pioneer spirit was generated based on both the new faith and the new extension of agricultural land into areas that were previously jungle. Because of the geographical changes taking place then, these newly available or newly cleared areas came with no pre-existing cultural baggage and it may be for this reason that Islam took root here more easily than in the western part, which had a much longer history of settled population.

The insistent presence of water, whether as the waterways of the rivers or the brackish seaways of the delta, has deeply influenced all aspects of traditional life in Bengal especially in the areas of agriculture, diet and commercial activity. Rice is the staple diet and at least two crops a year are possible; the delta has one of the highest population densities in the world. Tales concerning the fruitfulness or otherwise of the rice crop are, not surprisingly, common (see the stories of both Manasa and Kamalekamini, pp. 60–66, where the goddess is envisaged as a full golden pot, a symbol of luscious fertility), and

although the potential fertility of eastern India is great, famines have also been a feature of life, the most recent and devastating example being in 1943. Diet in Bengal is also determined by the presence of water, as fish is the item most usually eaten with rice; this is the case whether the fish is caught in fresh or sea water (the former is considered more

Detail from an embroidered cotton coverlet, or kantha, depicting fishes. Probably from eastern Bengal, now Bangladesh, late 19th/early 20th century.

'sweet'). The lore around fish is extensive and the lengths to which Bengalis will go to secure their favourite variety, be it ilish (hilsa) fish or freshwater prawns, are legendary. Again, this close connection with the life of the waters is reflected in Bengali narratives, and concomitantly with the visualization of them. 'Messing around in boats', always considered a foible of the English, is in the riparian parts of Bengal and in the delta an overriding interest – indeed requirement – and the numbers of different types of vessels, for fishing, for transport or for pleasure, were and still are great.

Finally, on the subject of the waterways and seaways, it is clear that from very early times, at least from the beginning of the Christian era, the mouths of the delta have provided harbours and landing stages from which international trade could be carried out. This is recorded in the Greek geographical text known as *The Periplus of the Erythraean Sea* and in a list of port names in Ptolemy's *Geography*. The ports include 'Gange' and 'Tamalates', which may be identified with modern Chandraketugarh and Tamluk (the latter seems quite certain; for both see map, p. 6). In urban entrepôts such as these the products of the Ganges valley could be assembled (especially textiles) and exchanged for a large range of incoming articles. Later, in the medieval period, there was clearly also much sea-going activity based on the eastern India–South-East Asia axis. This trade route linked eastern India with all the Indian-influenced centres on the South-East Asia coast, from the city of Dhanyawadi in Arakan in the north to Borobudur on the island of Java in the south and via the many cities and settlements in what are now the states of Burma, Thailand, Malaysia, Cambodia and Vietnam, where Indian culture spread with such astonishing speed in the first millennium AD. The growth of Buddhism in these areas, although organized in the first instance from south India, was more closely linked to eastern Indian culture in the Pala period (eighth to twelfth centuries AD) and was made especially poignant by the presence in this part of India of the holy sites of pilgrimage, the places connected with the life story of the Buddha. One of the constants of Buddhist expansion was its link with commerce – its proponents were more usually merchants than kings – and this adventurousness in the commercial arena seems to have continued in eastern India even after Buddhism declined in the late medieval period. As with other river-based activity, the mercantile aspect of life is represented in the narratives of the Bengalis. Merchants trading as far as Sri Lanka were still being sung of and illustrated right into the nineteenth century (see pp. 65–7). Given the rich commercial background of eastern India, it is not surprising that the London-based East India Company was drawn to Bengal in the late seventeenth century, along with trading companies from a number of other countries, and that it grew here from being merely a trading company to being a ruler of a vast and wealthy territory.

A rich merchant's ocean-going ship under sail. Detail from a painted scroll telling the story of the Muslim saint Gazi, Bengal, c.1800. For other registers from this same scroll, see pp. 68–72.

Brief history of Bengal

Bengal only enters history with the remarkable, though chance, discovery at Mahas-thangarh, in modern Bangladesh, of a small, inscribed stone tablet (second to third century BC). It bears six lines written in *brahmi* script, the earliest of the Indian scripts. It provides us with the ancient name of Pundranagara (now Mahasthangarh), as well as a suggestion that the inscription may have been a fragment from a larger one of the type associated with the great Emperor Ashoka, whose rock-cut epigraphs found throughout the subcontinent show him to have been much influenced by the peaceful ideals of Buddhism. If this interpretation is correct, it also marks the first appearance in Bengal of Buddhism, which was – over the next 1500 years – to have such a pro-found effect on the whole region.

Although an illuminating discovery, this small inscribed slab from Mahasthangarh is a sole find and thus difficult to use as a source for elaborate extrapolation. Archaeological evidence from other sites, such as Chandraketugarh, bring the story of civilization in Bengal into the present era, but there is little continuous narrative until the time of the second of the great pan-Indian empires of antiquity, that of the Guptas of the fourth and fifth centuries AD. Both northern and western Bengal were probably included in their domain, and during this period the long sequence of inscriptions on copper plates that are such a feature of medieval India begin to appear. These mostly record the granting of land but coincidentally often include historical information such as the names of kings and localities. The first of the Bengal sequence is dated to c. AD 433, and they continue until the arrival in eastern India of Muslim dynasts in the early thirteenth century.

This long period, from the end of the Guptas until the arrival of Islam, saw powerful dynasties emerge who ruled throughout much of northern and eastern India. As far as Bengal was concerned, the most important were rulers from the Pala and the Sena dynasties, while in south-eastern Bengal the Devas and the Chandras held sway. The Palas were in power between the late eighth and the twelfth centuries, not only in Bengal but also in the neighbouring region of Bihar. During Pala rule Buddhism flourished, and its most holy site – Bodh-Gaya (the place where the Buddha achieved Enlightenment) – lay within the Pala domain. The Palas were important patrons of architecture, painting and, above all, sculpture in both stone and bronze. This was a period of great sophistication and accomplishment in eastern India, a fact reflected in the accounts left by Tibetan pilgrims. It was also a time when contacts with lands beyond India become highly developed; trade and cultural connections, especially in the service of Buddhism, were maintained throughout South-East Asia and China (by sea), as well as with Tibet (by land). The following dynasty, the Senas, who ruled during the twelfth century, continued the earlier traditions but mostly favoured Hindu cults rather than the previous Buddhist ones. This change mirrors what was happening in much of the rest of India, where devotional, personal cults that had originated in southern India were becoming more and more influential (see p. 47).

The Sena dynasty came to a dramatic end when Turkish adventurers unexpectedly defeated Lakshmanasena, the last of his line, in 1204. They were themselves the advance troops of the army that only ten years previously had invaded north-west India, establishing Muslim dominion in India for the first time. Among these first Muslim troops were Turks, Afghans, Persians and Arabs, all keen to participate in the wealth of eastern India. Bengal continued to be ruled from the old Sena capital of Lakhnauti (later known as Gaur) in

Mihrab panel, probably from Gaur, northern Bengal. The sculptors employed by both Hindu and Muslim rulers drew on the same rich reservoir of decorative motifs, including full-blown lotus bosses, vegetal scrolls and hanging lamps, all of which are seen here. Late 15th century.

north-western Bengal. The governors here were themselves viceroys for the new Muslim rulers of northern India in far-off Delhi; they broke away only in 1338. These independent sultans continued until the Mughal conquest of eastern India by Akbar (from 1576 onwards), and this period saw the consolidation of Islam in the region with the development of a distinctive architecture in brick decorated with coloured tilework. Bengali literature also began to establish itself at this time, patronized by the sultanate rulers. They had no interest in the older Sanskrit traditions but saw that the everyday stories of their people, written in the indigenous language, were worth supporting. These new, local narratives became known as the *Mangalkavya* literature. Examples from this large corpus are discussed later and typically include the legends of local deities, especially those of Manasa and Chandi (pp. 60–66). A distinctively Bengali culture developed during this period when local and incoming influences combined to produce a unique synthesis. In the late sixteenth century Saiyid Sultan wrote his remarkable poem *Nabi Bangsa*, which has been described 'as a kind of "national religious epic" for Bengali Muslims' (Michell, *Islamic Heritage of Bengal*, p. 31). This astonishing act of syncretism presents the different forms of the Hindu gods along with biblical and Qur'anic figures – including Muhammad – in a single developmental line. Pragmatic tolerance was clearly at work here, allowing the ancient local beliefs to be included in the new dispensation.

This period of local development came to an end when eastern India was once again ruled from Delhi, by the Mughals (from the late sixteenth to the eighteenth centuries). The capital moved eastwards to Dhaka – due to the silting up of the channels, Gaur had become difficult to reach by river – and was adorned with buildings of a type found in similar provincial capitals of the Mughal empire. As a province of the empire, Bengal thrived and then suffered, following the fortunes of the empire elsewhere. However, the major difference, compared with the rest of the empire, was the appearance in the delta from the late sixteenth century onwards of European traders. The presence of these foreigners – apart from the Portuguese, they included Dutch, French, Danish and British – was to have the most profound influence on eastern India, as indeed on the whole of the subcontinent. What began as a trading enterprise ended as an empire, but before that came about, eastern India was to slip out of the control of the Mughals and into the hands of local Muslim rulers. These were initially still based at Dhaka but then at Murshidabad, upstream of Calcutta, the settlement that had already by the time of these last independent rulers developed as the centre of British activity.

The British traders, members of the East India Company, were the last but also eventually the most successful of the European trading groups in India. Their earliest efforts were in Gujarat and in Madras, but Bengal offered outstanding possibilities for trade, as not only did it have access to a rich immediate hinterland, where textiles of famous quality were produced, but it was also located at the end of the major trans-Indian trade route provided by the Ganges river system. The whole of the commerce of northern India was available via this route. Furthermore, it was far from the centre of Mughal power in Delhi and consequently, as the old power decayed throughout the eighteenth

Detail from a large embroidered coverlet made for the Portuguese market, showing hunting scenes with European figures and, in the quadrant, an episode from a classical myth (the Death of Actaeon) copied from a European print. Probably made at Satgaon, Bengal, early 17th century.

century, the fortunes of the East India Company increased. The Battle of Plassey in 1757 brought to an end the dominance of the independent rulers at Murshidabad and saw the continuing rise of British power. For a further hundred years the Company – still based in Calcutta – continued its territorial expansion. However, the realities of government and the exercise of political power, alongside and often in conflict with the demands of trade, meant that the Company had finally to relinquish its authority to the Crown for the last hundred years of British rule. From the 1850s trade gave way to government and until 1911 this was from Calcutta (in this year the capital was moved to Delhi). The British period came to an end in 1947, hastened on its way by the agitation and intellectual ferment of the educated and wealthy middle class who resented their inability to control their own destinies. Bengal played a prominent role in this process far out of proportion to its size. The writings of authors such as Bankimchandra Chatterji (1838–94) – his novel *Anandamath* of 1880/81 included the famous rallying hymn 'Bande Mataram' – and, slightly later, Rabindranath Tagore (1861–1941) provided further intellectual basis for freedom from foreign rule. Tagore, while not a radical, was an undoubted nationalist, and the international recognition he gained (Nobel Prize for Literature in 1913 along with many later acknowledgements) was evidence for all to see that the intellectual arguments for freedom had impressive

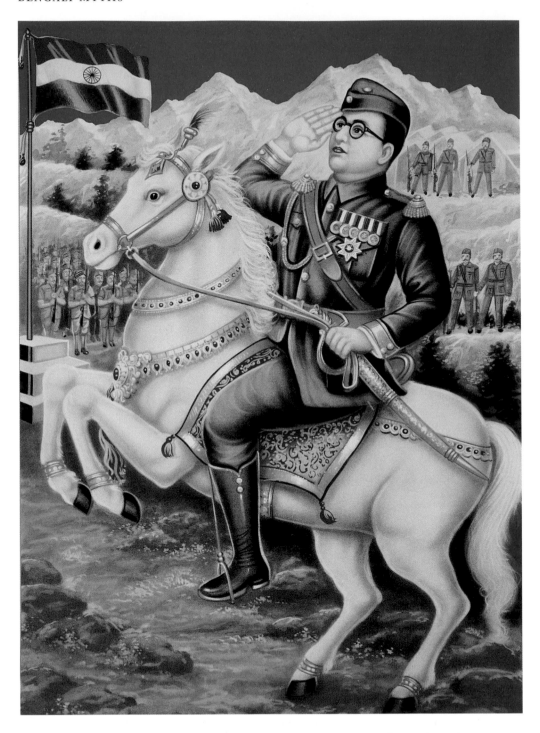

Popular print of Subhas Chandra Bose, known as Netaji ('Leader'), saluting the Indian tricolour. He founded the Indian National Army and fought with the Japanese against the British during the Second World War. Late 20th century.

foundations. Tellingly, though, Tagore himself said that he was the product of three civilizations, Hindu, Muslim and British. Other Bengali nationalists were more committed to direct and sometimes violent action, and the names of Subhas Chandra Bose and Aurobindo Ghosh are remembered today as fearless examples of this type. As the focus of still orally transmitted stories, they are on the way to becoming the subject of myths.

This last phase of Bengal's history has, like all periods of intense contact with outside groups, had a profound effect on local culture. It ranges from the frivolous, such as the etymology of the popular sweetmeats known as 'ladikannis' (named after Lady Canning, the wife of an early nineteenth-century Governor-General and an admirer of Indian cuisine), to the absolutely fundamental, such as the use of the English language, which has since colonialism become the current world lingua franca.

Independence also saw the partition of Bengal and the creation, initially, of the state of East Pakistan along with West Pakistan many hundreds of miles to the west. This situation of division became intolerable, and in 1971 the old state of East Pakistan became a separate and independent country renamed Bangladesh – the country of the Bengalis. Meanwhile, West Bengal, though cut off politically from the rest of Bengal, is still an important state with its capital of Calcutta (now also known as Kolkata) recognized – at least by its inhabitants – as the cultural hub of India.

Bengal's rich narrative heritage

Like so many other parts of India, Bengal has a rich legacy of orally transmitted narrative. Some of this material has over the centuries found its way into the corpus of written and eventually published literature. However, the majority has only been gathered together in anthologies of folk literature in recent centuries – or indeed has never been collected and is still only passed on orally. This is the case, especially, in non-urban communities, and not only among tillers of fields and tenders of flocks (nevertheless a huge number) but also among the fishermen and boatmen so plentiful in the delta landscape. Another strand of orally transmitted literature has been the preserve of women, who have over the centuries passed it from mother to daughter, reciting or singing stories in entirely domestic and non-commercial contexts – around the hearth at night or at rights of passage such as after childbirth. Yet other storytellers have lived by their narrative presentations, just as a few still do today on the crowded trains or buses that bring commuters into the cities of the region. This varied and potent reservoir of myths is now rapidly disappearing on account of the prevalence and increasing popularity in Bengal – as throughout the subcontinent – of television, cinema and video entertainment, all of which fulfil the same function as the ancient narratives, though the medium is quite different and the national and indeed international scope is much greater.

The long-standing legacy of oral exposition is founded on a mixture of the historical and cultural strands that make up Bengal's heritage. They include elements from its Buddhist, Hindu and Muslim past, all of which have provided Bengal with its stimulating narrative history. In a society that has, until only recently, been entirely dependent on its own indigenous resources for entertainment and for the transfer of lore, a range of forms has evolved for the dissemination of religious, morally uplifting or, frankly, just adventurous stories. These include dance, drama and singing, as well as less obvious media such as architectural decoration, which acts as a prompt for narration (the terracotta tile-work of the Bishnupur temples is a case in point). However, the most important mode of transmission has been oral, as described above. In this respect one of the most interesting, both aurally and visually, has been declaimed narration in conjunction with a painted scroll. In this method the episodes of the story being presented can be shown in correct sequence on the scroll, which is unwound by the singer using one hand, and wound up by him using the other. These singers were invariably male and this was their means of livelihood, travelling from village to village and soliciting payment in exchange for presenting their brightly coloured and beautifully illustrated tales of enchantment and wonder; in a few cases, and much truncated, this still occurs in parts of Bengal today.

Of special interest is the fact that these scrolls were painted and used, and the stories they told consumed, by people from both the Muslim and the Hindu communities, and in the more remote past no doubt by Buddhists as well. This illustrates a special characteristic of the religious life of Bengal, especially at the rural level, where aspects of all the different religious traditions have existed side by side and have frequently been mutually influential. The position of both the painters and the storytellers reflects this element of cross-over, as they are usually of low caste and historically have tailored their narratives to suit their audience – emphasizing the activities of a Muslim saint if singing in a Muslim village or the exploits of one of the Hindu heroes if in a majority Hindu village. Even their own family nomenclature reflects this ambiguity and they have both Hindu and Muslim names, which they use according to the circumstances.

The history and distribution of scroll-painting in India

Due to both the material from which they have been made (paper or cloth) and their use (involving frequent handling), scroll-paintings from the remote past have not survived. However, clues as to their existence can be gained from ancient texts. The grammarian Patanjali, writing in the second century BC, appears to mention in his commentarial work, the *Mahabhasya*, storytellers who used paintings as aids in presenting their narratives. This occurs in his discussion of when in a sentence one should use the tense known as the historical present. Later writers throughout the medieval period allude to storytellers with scroll-paintings, thus indicating that this ancient form of narration continued to thrive. The technique, like so much else in ancient Indian lore, travelled out of the subcontinent along with the teachings of the Buddha during the early to middle centuries of the first millennium AD. Another glimpse of the Indian tradition of storytelling scrolls is provided by the Buddhist paintings recovered from Central Asia at the beginning of the twentieth century, where conditions of survival – compared to India – have been much better. Here the didactic quality of paintings in the service of Buddhism is very clear. Similarly, at the end of the first millennium the apostles of Tibet, coming from the great centres of Buddhist learning in India, including Bengal, carried with them painted scrolls as aids in teaching the new faith. These were the ancestors of the distinctive painted hangings of the Tibetan tradition, *thang-kas*, and are culturally close cousins to the painted scrolls of Bengal.

Returning to India, these traditions of recitation accompanied by pictorial presentation are found in many of the different cultures of the subcontinent. Bengal is not the only inheritor of this idea, with well-known traditions of narrative scroll-painting recorded from Andhra Pradesh, Gujarat and Nepal, while related examples – large rectangular cloths with painted registers of narrative – are known from Rajasthan, Tamil Nadu and Sri Lanka.

Storyteller, or patua, *demonstrating the use of a painted scroll to accompany recitation. This example shows ten-headed Ravana in an episode from the* Ramayana. *Ahmdabad village, Midnapore District, West Bengal, early 1990s.*

21

Storytelling scrolls in Bengal

If Buddhism was present in Bengal during the time of Ashoka (third century BC), it is likely that storytellers with scroll-paintings illustrating their tales were also present, travelling the countryside and telling the moral stories in which were embedded the teachings and values of the new system. The missionary zeal of Buddhism seems to have been an influential element in the development of storytelling with pictorial aids. In the early centuries after the death of the Buddha in the fifth century BC Buddhist monks continued his injunction on them to be itinerant. This, combined with the need for the monk-teachers to explain moralities such as the Life of the Buddha and the stories of the master's previous lives (the Jataka Tales), can account for the rise in the Indian context of the travelling storyteller accompanied by explanatory pictorial representations. The claim must, though, remain speculation, as no examples of such painted aids survive from the period of Ashoka.

The history of these fascinating objects in the late middle ages is obscure and we can only pick up the story again with actual surviving examples. Today these earliest records are held in only a handful of institutions around the world. Probably none of them can be dated much before c.1800, although no exact date can be given as none are inscribed. Comparative stylistic analysis is the only way to suggest a dating for these documents, and similarities with late Mughal painting provide the tentative date quoted above. One feature they all have in common is their enormous length. The most important example in the British Museum, which appears to deal with the stories of the Muslim saints Gazi and Manik, is – despite being incomplete at both ends – still more than 13 metres (42 feet) long and has fifty-four individual registers. Indeed, the early twentieth-century scholar Gurusaday Dutt wrote (quoted in Dallapiccola, *Shastric Traditions in Indian Arts*, p. 432): 'In Eastern Bengal the expression *Gazir pat* is in common parlance synonymous with excessive and inordinate length, from which it may be presumed that these scroll paintings used to be of considerable length in olden times.' They share with their modern cinematic counterparts a concern with audience seduction, using extra scenes, diversions, colourful escapades and the like to encourage the engagement of the audience. They are designed to excite the viewer and operate in the same way that the very best Indian paintings do, relying on colour, emotion and fantasy to heighten the otherwise mundane lives of the audience.

Excitement, colour and length are, therefore, predominant features of the storytelling tradition of India and ones that will appear frequently in the examination of Bengali narratives to follow. The essential aural element of storytelling, which in Bengal often involves chanting in a distinctively high voice, cannot – unfortunately – be included here but it should always be borne in mind when reading the stories or viewing the images used in their presentation.

The Goddess Durga

Historical background

The story of Durga has been known in the Indian subcontinent for nearly 2,000 years, perhaps longer. Depictions of her in her most characteristic form of killing the buffalo-demon, Mahisha, are to be found dating from at least the Kushan period of the first centuries AD in the Mathura area of northern India. The iconography, though, of this climactic moment in her myth was not fixed until somewhat later, and it has been argued that the earliest representations of Durga from Bengal – terracotta and stone plaques from the Mahasthangarh area in Bangladesh – illustrate a stage in the standardization of this imagery. In these early images from Bengal (between the third and sixth centuries AD), as also those from north India, the act in the myth depicted precedes one that later became standard. The demon appears in full buffalo form, while the goddess grapples with or stands above it. One of her feet is placed on the neck of the beast, and she prepares to behead it. Other versions of this image are known from elsewhere in India during the first millennium, as is testified by a sculpted panel at Udayagiri in the Vidisha region. This and other panels in the man-made cave are dated by an inscription to AD 401. In the Durga panel she is shown with twelve arms and holds the buffalo-demon by its hind legs while trampling on its head, which lies on the ground; this form also does not survive into later common use.

The veneration of the goddess spread far from the first north Indian examples. In the seventh-century sculpted panels at Mahabalipuram in Tamil Nadu, southern India, the notion of a victorious goddess defeating a buffalo-demon is well established. Here in one of the great masterpieces of Indian sculpture – again as part of a man-made cave construction – she appears in the shrine now named after her battle with the demon, the Mahishasuramardini Cave. The iconography differs, though, from that seen in the north: Durga rides on her lion as if on a horse, while Mahisha has a buffalo head but is otherwise human bodied. The more common and longer-lasting image of the goddess in southern India shows her standing on the head of the decapitated buffalo; in these visions of her the battle has already taken place.

All these examples of the still-evolving iconography of the goddess hail from different parts of the subcontinent. In depictions from the beginning of the second millennium, however, the killing of the buffalo has already occurred, and the demon – now in human form and issuing from the neck of the decapitated buffalo – is speared by the goddess from above. This is the form that has such an enduring popularity in eastern India, above all in Bengal.

Perhaps the most important element in the crystallization of the Durga image and its dissemination was the text that, so far as can be determined today, first elaborated her myth; this is the *Devi Mahatmya*, now surviving within the much larger text of the *Markandeya Purana*. The *Devi Mahatmya* dates from the fifth to sixth century AD and contains several stories about the goddess, including that of Durga as killer of the buffalo-demon and that of Durga's generation of the goddess Kali and Kali's later activities on the battle-field. These two myths are described below.

Whether the legend of the victorious goddess relates to any historical event is unclear. Is the defeat of the demon merely an expression of an overall belief in the triumph of good over evil, or does it reflect the defeat of a people or a sect who are represented by the buffalo? These questions are difficult to decide, but one scholar has recently pointed out that many medieval texts that would later become canonical Hindu works (the *Puranas*) revolve around conflict with another group and are filled with violence. This analysis continues by speculating that in such myths we have a record of the defeat of heterodox groups such as Buddhists and Jains, who in the late centuries BC and early centuries AD were the dominant religious forces in the Indian subcontinent. Is the story of Durga's defeat of the buffalo-demon an example of conflict between orthodox and heterodox groups? Such an explanation is intriguing but is today almost impossible to prove. Yet other scholars have pointed out that the animal associated with incoming Indo-Aryan groups in the second millennium BC is the cow and that the buffalo is indigenous to India. Could the Durga myth therefore represent a victory of the incomers over the original inhabitants? Further, in Hindu mythology the buffalo is the vehicle of the god of death, Yama, and so, by conquering the buffalo-demon, Durga can perhaps be seen as conquering death itself. While fascinating to probe, such theories are now also difficult to prove.

Durga and Kali in Bengal: history and characteristics

In eastern India (Bengal and Bihar) early traces of Durga are few despite the couple of examples mentioned above, from Mahasthangarh. It is not until the later medieval period that she comes into her own in the sculpture of the Pala-Sena period of the eighth to twelfth centuries AD. In the post-medieval period, though, she has a special place and an extended mythology in eastern India, where her story overlaps with, and includes that, of other deities. She also appears in Bengal under various names, of which Durga (literally, 'the inaccessible') is only one of the most important. She is certainly thought of as being one and the same as Parvati or Uma, the wife of Shiva, although in the latter manifestation she is a more demure and dependent figure; as Durga, she is the centre of action and of attention and everyone else in the scheme is secondary.

Popular print of the goddess Durga in the form she is worshipped at Durga Puja in Bengal. Lithograph, Bengal Art Studio, Calcutta, c.1895.

While Durga is not the same as the other well-known goddess of Bengal, bloodthirsty Kali (literally, 'the Black One'), both are – in Bengal – conceived of as goddesses of battle and also, paradoxically, as mothers. Further, the legend of Kali's birth, which is recorded in the third part of the *Devi Mahatmya*, points up this closeness between the two deities, since she is imagined as having been created from the personified anger of the ferocious Durga as she faces the demons. The story, which in this final part of the *Devi Mahatmya* revolves around the demons Shumbha and Nishumbha and is of a type common in myths about Durga, concerns the time when the gods are at the mercy of demons and call on the goddess Durga to help them. She appears before them as a beautiful girl who is then desired by the demons. It is their lust for her that sets up their demise and, after several attempts to secure her, they finally send in their generals Chanda and Munda. At this point the beautiful goddess explodes in anger, and out of her blackened forehead bursts forth the ferocious and utterly terrifying Kali, who quickly gobbles up all the demon army. Finally, both demon kings are destroyed by the black goddess. Kali is described in the text as grotesque and frightening and in Bengal is invariably depicted as four-armed (one hand holds a decapitated head), garlanded with a necklace of human heads and wearing a girdle made up of the hands and arms of her victims. Equally terrifyingly, she sports earrings made of the bodies of dead children, has a lolling tongue dripping with sacrificial blood and keeps her mass of wavy black hair unloosed and falling down her back (this is always a sign in India of unfettered female power).

Kali is known to haunt cremation grounds where she is accompanied by an inauspicious dog, who jumps up to lick at the severed head she carries in one hand. She is also frequently depicted in eastern India as running out of control on the battlefield, crazed with blood-lust. She tramples all the cosmic enemies underfoot and, so the story goes, causes the whole universe to be rocked by her triumphant trumpeting and rage. Finally, she is only brought under control, and order restored to the world, when the rest of the gods request her husband Shiva to intervene (as Kali is a form of Durga, Shiva is considered her consort). The only way he is eventually able to distract her from her blood-lust is to lie down in front of her on the battlefield. Suddenly aware that she is angrily striding over the body of her own dear lord, she comes to a juddering halt, and the universe is saved.

Yet, despite all this horrifying battlefield imagery, Kali is nevertheless addressed as 'Ma' or 'Mother' and described as a goddess of great beauty. To non-Bengalis this is a strange concept, but this is how her devotees have envisaged her. The poet Ramprasad Sen (*c.*1718–75) wrote famously and ecstatically of her thus, combining many ideas in his vision of her – as a denizen of the battlefield, as a ghoulish blood-stained inhabitant of the cremation ground, and as a saviour. The saint Ramakrishna (1836–86), who lived at the Dakshineshvar temple, north of Calcutta, also addressed and worshipped her as 'Mother', envisaging himself as a child before her. Ramakrishna, who was lost in devotion to the goddess Kali, venerated her pre-eminently in the form where she strides over the body of recumbent Shiva; this is the image of her enshrined at Dakshineshvar. There are many stories about his vision of female divinity

*Popular print of the goddess Kali on the battlefield striding
over recumbent Shiva. Lithograph, Chore Bagan Art Studio,
Calcutta, c.1895.*

and its interpretation by his followers. One relates to the Belur temple, the world headquarters of the Ramakrishna Mission, which was founded by Ramakrishna's disciple Swami Vivekananda (1863–1902) to make known his master's message internationally. Here they tell how each year the goddess herself is made manifest in a young girl child of pre-pubescent age, who for one day is offered homage through a special puja ('worship'), the Kumari Puja, and honoured by tens of thousands of devotees.

The two elements of Durga's story in Bengal

The two most important stories told about Durga in eastern India are intertwined, especially at the time of her annual festival, Durga Puja in the month of Ashvin (September/October); the exact days of the Puja differ each year and are determined by priestly astrologers. To an outsider the two major elements of Durga's story in Bengal appear contradictory. One, the tale of Durga defeating the buffalo-demon, Mahisha, is martial and cosmic in character and is pan-Indian. The other, meanwhile, is pacific, family centred and specifically Bengali, and concerns the return of the goddess Durga to her family home, escaping for a few precious days from the tyranny of her wild and unpredictable husband Shiva, who is left behind in the Himalayan fastness of their home on Mount Kailash. Both of these stories are invoked and reconciled at the Puja, the ten-day period during which Durga is honoured and which is the most important of the religious observances among Hindus in eastern India. This is the time when devotees come face to face with Durga, as for the rest of the year she is not present with them. Almost without exception Durga is not the focus of temple worship in Bengal; temples in which she is enshrined as a major deity are rare. This absence in the physical realm is reflected in the mythological one: she is not present, as she is dutifully acting out her role as wife to Lord Shiva, far away in the Himalayas. In this respect Durga is unlike Kali, with whom she is similar in other ways, for Kali is enshrined in temples, famously in Calcutta at Kalighat (this name provides the popular etymology for the name of the city itself) and at Dakshineshvar, north of Calcutta (where Ramakrishna worshipped her). Durga, however, has none of this exposure. Her great moment is the period of the Puja: she comes, she receives the adoration of her followers and then she leaves, until the cycle comes around next year. This cyclical quality of her worship, which occurs after the harvest has been brought in, recalls the agricultural and fertility origins of at least part of her complex personality, as does the gifting to her of blood offerings (usually goats, though replaced more often today, and especially among Vaisnavas – followers of Vishnu – by a symbolic gourd).

The celebration of Durga Puja in Bengal: history and modernity

Both of the two strands of narrative – Durga in her cosmic form killing the buffalo-demon, and the goddess in her domestic form as daughter of the house returning to her loving family – come together in the ten-day long Bengal festival of Durga Puja. This is celebrated wherever significant numbers of Bengalis are found, be it in London, Washington or Kuala Lumpur, but most significantly in Bengal and pre-eminently in the city of Calcutta. The history of the Puja in the city indicates a trajectory from private and wealthy celebration in the eighteenth and nineteenth centuries to public and democratic involvement throughout the city in the twentieth and twenty-first centuries. Today all quarters of the city construct their image of the goddess and indeed compete to produce the most interesting, magnificent or innovative one, each housed in a fantastic, temporary tented pavilion called a *pandal*. During the Puja days these *pandals* are visited by hordes of people engaged in the part-religious but mostly social activity of 'pandal-hopping', assessing the qualities of the images and the artistry of the *pandal*, especially as some topical subject is frequently taken as the basis for each *pandal* construction. For instance, in the 2005 Puja one *pandal* was based on the tsunami disaster in South-East Asia earlier that year, and others dealt with environmental issues, which are increasingly dominating informed discussion in India. These topics are also often elaborated in flashing light displays in the nearby streets. *Pandal*-hopping in the final days of the Puja carries on into the early hours and is complemented by the throbbing accompaniment of *dhakis*, the typical drummers of the Puja celebrations, who come in from the countryside and give bravura performances in the *pandals* using large, shoulder-held drums that are decorated with feather plumes. They are often accompanied by a musician with a small plate-like gong, the *kasar*. The ten-day period of the Puja starts slowly but ends in three or four days of tumultuous holiday when the whole city is *en fête*.

The history of the first Puja celebrations in Bengal is now lost, but most scholars accept an initial date for the earliest festivities some time in the early seventeenth century, associated with *zamindari*, or land-owning families, above all the Maharajas of Navadvip with their seat at Krishnanagar. These events were undoubtedly possible only in the courts of the rulers who could spare the resources needed to fund the substantial costs of making the image and providing the services of the priestly community to perform the rituals during the days of the celebration – let alone pay for the musicians, lights, garlands, sweetmeats and food for all those taking part. What is much more certain is that, by the time of the rise of the city of Calcutta as a major urban centre in the eighteenth century, the Puja had become a social as well as religious event, when status and wealth were displayed in the most opulent manner. Further, while it was unquestionably a Hindu religious festival, it also became an occasion for rich Hindus to welcome their British political and commercial counterparts and display the lavish quality of their households. The great houses of wealthy Hindus in north Calcutta vied with each other to put on increasingly elaborate Puja events (see illustration p. 32). Famously, Robert Clive was invited to celebrations to mark the presence in Calcutta of the goddess of victory (that is, Durga at her Puja) immediately after his victory at Plassey in 1757 over the last ruler of independent Bengal, Nawab Siraj-ud-Daulah of Murshidabad. Here history and myth collide.

Durga as the goddess of victory

In the texts the story of the triumph of Durga over the forces of cosmic disintegration is drawn out and elaborate, but over the centuries, and in different regional traditions, a fundamental core narrative with variations has developed. This basic story, which is known in Bengal just as it is elsewhere in India, goes as follows.

Back in the mists of cosmic time demons forced the gods to grant them favours. This was achieved by the demons practising intense yogic exercises, thereby building up for themselves huge reserves of merit. Eventually, the demons received so many favours for their austerities that they were able to rule the world; indeed, in some cases the gods in heaven were beholden to them. One by one, the deities were forced to request aid from ever higher beings; their armies had been completely annihilated. Finally, there was no one left in the divine hierarchy to whom the world – human or divine – could appeal. When they were faced with this apparently terminal situation, the combined fear and anger of the greatest of the gods coalesced in an epiphany of frightening and brilliant light – and the goddess Durga was born. Subsequently, each of the great gods armed her with one of their weapons, and she set forth, brandishing her newly acquired weapons, riding a lion mount and ready for battle with the chief demon. Little did the demon realize that his fate was finally sealed. He was enraged by the appearance of the goddess and sent his army of demons against her. When they were all killed or eaten by Durga's lion, he finally appeared himself. Raging through the universe, Durga and the demon affect the earth and the sea alike as they storm together in battle. At one point, in his attempt to destroy her, he changes his shape, becoming a lion, a man, an elephant and then a buffalo again. Now comes the moment when the goddess and the demon face each other in final, climactic battle. Durga lets out her spine-chilling battle cry, takes a last swig of intoxicating alcohol and battle is re-joined. Only to the demon is the result ever in doubt, and the goddess easily decapitates the buffalo. At this point the human-form demon issues from the neck of the beheaded buffalo, and Durga, almost nonchalantly, pierces him with her trident; the contest for cosmic sovereignty is concluded. She then graciously acknowledges the thanks of all the gods.

It is this final scene in the epic that is depicted in the images made for the Durga Puja and housed in the *pandals*: Durga standing in triumph, flanked by her children Ganesha, Karttikeya, Lakshmi and Sarasvati (in Bengali: Gonesh, Kartik, Lokki and Shoroshshoti). This final apotheosis is distinctively Bengali, for, while the first two gods can truly be considered the children of Durga – she is, after all, the fierce form of Shiva's consort Parvati and thus the parent of elephant-headed Ganesha and of the war-god Karttikeya – in no other tradition are the goddesses Lakshmi and Sarasvati thought of as her progeny. Their inclusion, however, provides symmetry and greater importance to the Durga tradition. In the impressive tableaux built each year for Durga Puja the moment of cosmic restabilizing and of triumphant victory is re-enacted and celebrated. She is the embodiment of the triumph of good over evil.

In the period leading up to Indian Independence in 1947 this aspect of victorious and righteous power personified had a special resonance in the annual creation of the Durga images in Calcutta. In these Mother India was seen to be vanquishing the forces of evil, understood as the colonial power, and her image became a rallying point around which patriots gathered. The *pandals* became the focus for anti-government agitation, and in one famous instance in Faridpur (now in Bangladesh) the figure of the demon Mahisha was replaced by that of a prone British military officer, while Subhas Chandra Bose, the political firebrand and freedom fighter, took the place of Ganesha and Karttikeya. While this is an extreme and remarkable example of the *pandals* being used for political purposes, almost all of them in today's Durga Puja celebrations in Calcutta have some sort of message to put over, whether of a political, social, environmental or cultural nature. The fact that Bose's life is now well on its way to 'canonization' and has its own iconography (see pp. 18–19) demonstrates the way in which history and legend combine to become myth.

The story of Durga's triumph is illustrated in countless depictions from Bengal. As the delta country is devoid of sources of stone for building or sculpture but is rich in clay, it is not surprising that this is the most widely used material for portraying the goddess, especially for the temporary images used in

Painted-clay pot lid, or sara, *depicting Durga defeating the demon Mahisha. Such items were traditionally used as inexpensive images of the goddess. Calcutta, 1980s.*

A Durga Puja image in a wealthy house in Calcutta in the 1790s. Lithograph reproduced over two pages in Balthazar Solvyns, Les Hindous, *vol. III, Paris, 1810.*

Durga Puja. Indeed, not only is clay plentifully available but is also associated here, as elsewhere in the subcontinent, with female deities and the fructifying power of Mother Earth, who either brings forth crops or terrifyingly denies them on account of drought, pestilence or flood. One of the earliest printed illustrations of Durga Mahishasuramardini, as she appears in the myth described above, is in the four-volume publication of the Flemish artist Balthazar Solvyns, *Les Hindous*. Solvyns lived in Calcutta from 1791 to 1803, and between 1808 and 1812 published his monumental work, richly illustrated with his own lithographs. Two double-page prints in it are relevant to the myth of the goddess Durga. The first depicts the Durga image, the *pratima*, as constructed in the house of a well-off Hindu family. It is slightly separate from the rest of the house, on the specially built platform for the worship of the goddess, the *thakur-dalan*, just as it is today (see frontispiece). The second of Solvyns's prints shows the culmination of the immediately following Puja in the calendar, that of the closely related goddess Kali. The final act of the Kali Puja takes the same form as for Durga Puja and is thus important to note here. The *pratima* is shown being taken out on the River Hooghly (a tributary of the Ganges) and, balanced on a plank between two boats, is consigned to the water as the two boats float apart from each other in midstream. She returns to the sacred river, the clay disintegrating in the water, and her devotees must wait for another year before they see her again. Such departures of Durga images are still seen in Calcutta today at the end of her Puja.

The image of the goddess Durga from the De household (one of the oldest family Pujas in Calcutta) is loaded on two boats so that it can be taken out onto the river for immersion, or visarjan. *Calcutta, 2005.*

The temporary quality of these clay figures – they were only ever made for the ten-day duration of the Puja – makes survivals from early periods rare. A painted plaque in the British Museum is perhaps the earliest extant example of a clay sculpture of the goddess Durga in the Bengali, Durga Puja form. It was already in the collection in 1845 and even in its now damaged state is a remarkable survival. In this tableau the multi-armed goddess is depicted at the moment of triumph. The basic clay material for the group has been covered with cloth and then painted, while the figures were separately modelled and then added. Following the myth as described above, the goddess is shown riding on her lion, defeating the demon and surrounded by her children. Above them, and uniting the whole ensemble, is the *chalchitra*, the arching painted

Painted-clay panel depicting Durga defeating the buffalo-demon. Bengal, before 1845.

scroll on which are painted other divine figures such as her husband Shiva, Krishna and dancing ascetics. Of interest today is the grouping of the deities on the clay plaque. In the nineteenth century this was the traditional way for them to be represented, but today the *chalchitra* has, for the most part, been abandoned and the deities are now shown as separate, individual figures, although they are still always smaller in size than the central and still dominating Durga. The 1845 example is also interesting as it shows the god Karttikeya in a form prior to his re-invention as a Calcutta dandy in the later nineteenth century. In the latter form, complete with large earrings, broad-brimmed hat and feather, and European-style shoes, he appears in late nineteenth-century depictions of this scene, including paintings made at the Kalighat temple, in Calcutta.

Examples of such clay images of Durga were made in the days running up to the festival and sold to devotees from stalls. A painting executed in the so-called Company style (pictures by Indian artists for European patrons, initially officers of the East India Company) provides a useful comparison and is illustrated below. It shows a seller of painted-clay images, including one of Durga Mahishasuramardini in typically Bengali style, and was probably produced in Patna just to the west of today's state of West Bengal in the mid-nineteenth century; it is thus roughly contemporary with the 1845 painted-clay image discussed above. A further variant, deliberately anachronistic, was created in London for the 1982 Festival of India in imitation of those made in ivory for the Great Exhibition of 1851, but on this occasion fashioned of pith of the shola reed and on a much larger scale; it is more than 8 feet (2.4 metres) tall.

Seller of painted-clay devotional images. Durga is on the top shelf at the right, while Kali striding over recumbent Shiva appears further along the same shelf. The potter/sculptor is depicted on the right. Watercolour, Patna, Bihar, c.1850.

Painted-clay image (detail) of the goddess Kali. She wears a garland of human heads and earrings of children's bodies. Probably made in Krishnanagar, Bengal, late 19th century.

Also of great historic importance because of their unlikely survival is a group of ten painted-clay sculptures of deities, including goddesses, which must have been made before 1894 when they came to the British Museum. It has been suggested that these were produced in Krishnanagar, an important centre for clay-image production following the settlement there of craftsmen from Natore by Maharaja Krishnachandra Ray (1710–83), the famous royal devotee of Kali and promoter of her cult who was instrumental in developing the Durga Puja as a major public ritual. Goddesses, including Kali (for her myth see pp. 24–8), Radha (see pp. 56–8) and Jagadhatri, are included in this group. Jagadhatri (the name means 'Mother of the World') is a closely related form of Durga and her myth, just like Durga's, concerns the defeat of armies of demons commanded by a mighty giant, here known as Jarasura. Like Durga, she saves the world from cosmic disintegration. Her most obviously distinguishing feature is that the lion on which she rides appears itself on an elephant. These wonderful clay images illustrating the myths of Bengal are important indicators of the work of nineteenth-century craftsmen who drew on traditions reaching back several centuries and whose descendants continue this ancient custom to this day.

The workshop of Nemai Chandra Paul, maker of clay images. Both craftsmen are preparing lengths of jute to be used for the hair of the goddess. The lion vehicle of another Durga image stands waiting to be painted on the left. Krishnanagar, Bengal, 2005.

The centre of clay-image making today in Calcutta is Kumartuli in the northern quarter of the city. Here the craftsmen mainly make images for the Pujas, above all for the Durga Puja in the autumn. All the many stages of production, from the first twisting of the rice-straw armature to the final dressing of the sculptures with tinsel and metal-sheet jewellery, take place here. When complete, the Puja images leave Kumartuli for their destinations in a logistical feat of astonishing, almost surreal character. Several thousand images are transported through this series of narrow lanes by the banks of the river. The nearby streets are filled with vehicles, from lorries to rickshaws, loaded with the towering temporary sculptures of the goddess and her retinue of four children. They speed through the city thoroughfares on their way to the *pandals,* a trajectory that is mirrored in less than a week when the images are taken to the banks of the Hooghly and consigned to the holy waters for final dissolution – the clay used in the sculpture returns from whence it came. The craftsmen at Kumartuli are probably descended from those who came to the city from Krishnanagar (the previous centre of this work under the patronage of Maharaja Krishnachandra), as Calcutta expanded in the eighteenth century.

Durga as the beloved daughter returning to her family

In the second Durga story the Uma/Parvati side of her character is emphasized. Here she is envisaged as pacific and maternal and is welcomed particularly by the women of the household, with domestic rituals of arrival. In this form she is thought of as the daughter of Himavant and Menaka, the presiding deities of the Himalayas (Parvati literally means 'daughter of the mountain'). Her poignant story mirrors that of many Bengali women and their family relationships, especially in past centuries. Uma, we learn from the poetry sung at the time of her arrival for the Puja (she is also, of course, at the same time martial Durga), was married young to the frightening, though no doubt exciting, Shiva, also lord of a mountain, that of Kailash far to the west of Bengal. He is known to be a drug-crazed ne'er-do-well, who leads poor young Uma a sorry dance; there is even present in the palace Shiva's second wife, the river goddess Ganga, with whom Uma has to cohabit; Menaka is horrified that her darling daughter has to suffer so. Far away in Kailash, Uma is separated from her loving family and the city that they rule over. Only once a year is the family reunited at the time of the Durga Puja, when Uma is honoured in a rather different form as the victorious goddess who defeats the buffalo-demon. The early separation from her family that Uma has to undergo, marrying an older and dissolute man (child-marriage was the norm for many girls up to the beginning of the twentieth century), is reflected in a haunting song from rural Bengal recorded at the beginning of the twentieth century by the folklore scholar Dineshchandra Sen and commented on by him as follows (note the inevitable imagery of the river):

As the boat carrying her passes through the stream that flows past the village, Gauri [literally, 'the fair', an epithet of Parvati and Uma and thus of Durga] says to the boat-man, 'Brother boat-man, ply your oars slowly, my mother is crying, let me hear her voice a little more; / Oh my brother boat-man, ply the boat slowly, my sisters are crying, let me catch their sound; / Oh brother boat-man do not ply your boat so fast, yet my brothers are crying, let me hear their voices a little more.' At the time she left home the relations were weeping, for she was a little girl and never stayed even a day away from her home ... The little girls after their marriage, went to their husbands' home and were subjected to the maltreatment of their sisters-in-law and mothers-in-law. This accounts for the tender pathos of such situations. (Sen, *Folk Literature of Bengal*, p. 257)

Each year the days of the Durga Puja are recognized as the time when Bengali families are reunited. This was especially so in the past when the daughters of the house, who for the rest of the year were separated from their natal home, returned for a few days of loving reunion. The story of Durga returning to Bengal from her Himalayan home of Mount Kailash is made more tender by the fact that in eastern India Shiva is frequently presented not only as a powerful ascetic and a cosmic force but also as a penniless and worthless wanderer, who for most of the year makes his wife's life difficult and uncomfortable on account of his drunken and dissolute lifestyle. He is frequently depicted in

The goddess Uma or Durga returns to her natal home. Oil painting on canvas, Bengal, c.1890.

paintings from the Kalighat shrine with eyeballs disappearing beneath his eyelids, indicating his intoxicated state. Durga's release for a few days into the doting care of her parents in the beautiful and luxuriant land of the Ganges delta is thus one full of delight and is a subject found in the repertoire of the Kalighat painters. The emotion engendered by the welcome, the *agamani*, given to the goddess on her return to Bengal, and then the concomitant and inevitably unhappy end of her time of visiting, the *vijaya* (literally, 'victory' of the goddess over the buffalo-demon but also indicating the end of her 'mission' for the whole year), constitute an important and symmetrical part of the whole Puja. Indeed, today, and ever since the inaugural broadcast on All India Radio by Birendra Krishna Bhadra in 1930, the arrival of the goddess is announced over the airwaves through the recitation of poems of welcome and devotion. This takes place before dawn on the first day of the Puja, known as Mahalaya, and is so popular that tapes and CDs of this heartfelt chant are sold in great numbers each year. When the goddess finally leaves at the end of the Puja, her devotees line the streets and sorrowfully say goodbye, calling on her to come again next year and bless their lives once more with her presence.

The rich vein of eighteenth- and nineteenth-century poetry that is used to welcome the goddess is mirrored in the painting shown above. Here the moment of return to beloved Bengal is depicted as told in myth and in poetry. Brightly painted in the foreground is the haloed goddess, jewelled and crowned in the distinctive Bengali form, with tall pointed headgear. She is seated on a lotus saddle-cover and rides on her lion *vahana*, or animal mount. She is greeted by her father Himavant, who is dressed in royal attire and advances towards her. The goddess carries in her lap her child, elephant-headed Ganesha, whose diminutive arms are held out towards his grandfather in a mirror gesture of greeting. Ganesha's presence here is appropriate – even essential – as his presence blesses this Puja. He is the remover of all obstacles to new projects and the guarantor of auspiciousness. To the left and behind Himavant, but full of emotion at the moment of welcome, is Uma's mother. She takes up the traditionally correct position indicating that – at least in the public domain – she is secondary in importance to her husband. Hovering in the doorway yet further behind are other members of the household, flanked by plantains, auspicious garlanded pots and fluttering mango leaves over the lintel, all indications of good fortune and welcome. One of these attendants carries a yak-tail fly-whisk, while another appears to blow on a conch, also a sign of welcome. The other figure in the foreground is dark-skinned Nandikeshvara, Shiva's bull mount in human form. He accompanies his lord's wife on her journey from Mount Kailash to her parents' home. Finally, at a quite different scale, in the upper right-hand corner of the painting, three of the other subsidiary figures of the Durga Puja are depicted. Flying on their bird mounts are the deities – from left to right, Lakshmi on her owl, Sarasvati on her swan and Karttikeya on his peacock – all descending to earth to take part in the Puja of the goddess, who in Bengal is considered to be their mother. These three deities, along with Ganesha, are traditionally shown as accompanying Durga in the Puja tableaux, which are the most obvious public manifestation of this festival.

This painting not only tells the pacific, familial part of the Durga Puja story but indicates that fascinating conjunction of Indian subject matter and European technique so typical of Bengal in the nineteenth and early twentieth centuries. The traditional medium of painting in the subcontinent – small-scale watercolour imaging on paper – has been abandoned in favour of the European style of oil paint on canvas. Further, the concepts of a distant and receding horizon, and the concomitant of perspective and differential size depending on distance from the viewer, have been used. However, the artist has not applied the rules of perspective in their entirety, as the depiction of the late Georgian architecture of the mansion, to which the goddess is being welcomed, demonstrates. For, while it reflects some of the magnificent buildings of eighteenth-century Calcutta (it was not known as the City of Palaces for nothing), the artist has included more of the building than would strictly have been possible, had he been forced to present it within the strict rules of perspective. The Indian system of showing a building in multiple forms – plan, elevation and even section all in the same painting – sometimes has many advantages when a complete view is desired (the later realization of this same fact by Cubist painters in Europe was probably unconnected with the Indian tradition). Finally, the way in which both the mountain and the woodland landscapes have been visualized suggests alpine scenes in Germany and Switzerland, printed depictions of which had found wide currency in India in the late nineteenth century and probably formed the basis of such views, rather than anything that might have been personally experienced by the Bengali artist.

Conclusion

The myths and narratives of the goddesses of Bengal, both Durga and Kali, give us a powerful insight into eastern Indian culture. Their celebratory festivals each autumn, Durga Puja and Kali Puja, still energize the Hindu populations of Bengal and are enjoyed as holidays by everyone. That the presence of the goddesses among them is felt to be revivifying is clear from the enthusiasm of the population generally and also from the fact that these deities still provide inspiration for artists as diverse as Shyamal Dutta Roy (born 1934) and the twentieth-century ascetic Sachidananda Sen. Meanwhile, in a more equivocal vein the great Bengali film-maker Satyajit Ray (1921–92) has responded to the Bengali obsession with the goddess in his film *Devi* (*The Goddess*; 1960), which is based on a narrative originally developed by Rabindranath Tagore. This dark tale reminds those who see it that the goddess, in this instance Kali, is to be found not only at the great festivals, but equally in the domestic context, and that she is both benign and malign. Wherever she is she demonstrates the reconciliation of opposites and the transience of all phenomenal existence. These dramatically divergent elements in the stories of the Bengali goddesses show that they cover all human experience. Their myths seem to be telling us that there is no aspect of human life where their presence cannot be felt.

The goddess Kali by Shyamal Dutta Roy. Pen and ink drawing, Calcutta, 1977.

Krishna, the Divine Youth

'Without Krsna there is no song'
(quoted in Kinsley, *The Sword and the Flute*, p. 77)

Introduction

Krishna is the beautiful, youthful, dark-skinned god who wears a yellow dhoti, has a garland of forest flowers hanging from his neck and plays intoxicatingly on the flute. He is revered throughout the Indian subcontinent. All the regions of this vast land have their own stories about him. A certain and extensive core of myth is common throughout, but Bengal is renowned for a special elaboration of the story and a heightened emotional sensibility around his name. The common narratives about Krishna seem, from an anthropological point of view, to represent the slow amalgamation throughout the first millennium AD of various but different ideas, eventually solidifying around this one figure. Listed simply, these narratives, which are part of the culture of eastern India just as much as of any other part of the subcontinent, are as follows.

The story of Krishna

The appearance on earth of Lord Krishna took place at Mathura, south of Delhi. He and his brother Balarama were born to Devaki and her husband Vasudeva. However, the uncle of Devaki, Kamsa, the evil King of Mathura, had received a prophecy that he would lose his throne to a child of his niece, and therefore tried to kill all her children (he was successful with the first six of these, but the last two, the divine children, escaped his efforts). Of these last two, Balarama was miraculously removed from his mother's womb and born to another woman, while Krishna was smuggled out of Mathura and given to foster-parents, Nanda and Yashoda. They brought him up in the nearby village of Vrindavana in the forests of Braj, along with his brother Balarama (in the Bengal stories Balarama acts as a counter-balance to Krishna and is shown with his attribute the horn, just as Krishna is shown with the flute).

Brass sculpture of the young cowherd Krishna playing the flute (the instrument itself is never shown in sculptures). On the underside of the base is a dedicatory inscription in Assamese. The red colouring on the eyes indicates that the image has been ritually used. Assam, 19th century.

In Vrindavana, an idyllic pastoral community, the baby Krishna flourished, developing into a naughty, yet beguilingly beautiful child. He was constantly being rebuked (but never too seriously), for he took the greatest delight in running amok in the village, stealing butter and finding pots of sweet curds to guzzle – he appeared to have an insatiable appetite. As he grew up, he and his companions took to the forest, spending hours running through the jungle, acting like animals and generally behaving as if they hadn't a care in the world.

The child Krishna crawling on his throne and triumphantly holding up a ball of butter.
Painting on paper from the Kalighat shrine in Calcutta, late 19th century.

As a handsome young man, Krishna defeated the many demons sent by his uncle to destroy him (Kamsa had by this time learnt that Krishna had survived his attempts to kill him). Among these monstrous enemies, many of whom came in animal form, were a giant snake Aghasura, a giant ass Dhenuka and a river snake Kaliya, who terrorized the good people of Vrindavana. In this last story Krishna jumped into the river Jumna and, after much thrashing around in the water baiting and teasing the multi-headed cobra demon, defeated it. This he did by climbing on to its hoods, which were upraised in anger, and dancing on them until – exhausted – the giant snake had to capitulate. This tale, in which dancing is the weapon of choice, reminds us that Krishna works his divine magic in play, or *lila*. Captivating music – above all from Krishna's own instrument, the flute – dance and the ecstatic emotion of happy and uncomplicated eroticism are the hallmarks of Krishna's eternal kingdom. This is no more so than in the Bengali vision of the divine land of Vrindavana where he resides and where every devotee hopes to find eternal habitation.

Krishna further demonstrated his power to the inhabitants of Vrindavana – they quickly became his followers – when he protected them from the anger of Indra, the king of the gods. Indra, the ancient god of the storm, had become offended by the way that Krishna's devotees no longer honoured him but instead focused only on the beautiful youth, Krishna. In a rage he sent a great monsoon storm to destroy the cowherds of Braj. In this extremity, though, they were protected by Krishna who miraculously lifted up – as if it were an umbrella – the mountain of Govardhan, thus protecting his followers and their herds from the destructive torrents of Indra's storm. As proof of his outstanding powers, he is usually shown holding up the massive mountain solely on one finger. The printmakers of Bat-tala in Calcutta produced popular depictions of this scene where the youthful saviour god is shown in Bengali form (see p. 46). In this version Krishna is attended by his elder brother Balarama, who is identified by the horn he carries. Mount Govardhan is shown with all its flora and fauna spilling out over the edges, fancifully yet forcefully conveying the astonishing quality of the god's intervention. For pilgrims to Vrindavana today, many of whom are Bengalis, a visit to the site regarded as the Govardhan mountain is an absolute necessity as they tour the sacred places.

Krishna's most famous activity in the forests of Vrindavana while he was still a youth concerns his erotic dalliance with the female cowherds, the *gopis*, and above all with one of them, Radha. As we will see later, this is the element of Krishna's story that was developed most substantially by Bengali poets and devotees and is the great legacy of Bengali involvement in the cult of Krishna; killing demons, defeating gods and uprooting evil kings, all of these are secondary to Krishna's love-play with Radha. First, however, come those stories about Krishna and all the *gopis* together, and only when these are told, can Radha, alone with Krishna, be considered.

Krishna lifting up Mount Govardhan. Hand-coloured metal-cut print probably produced in Bat-tala, north Calcutta; writing in English along the top of the print (not shown) and the style of ornament suggest a date early in the 19th century.

Krishna summons his young female followers to join him in the forest for singing, dancing and dalliance through the sensuous playing of his flute; this is his messenger. On one famous occasion, while the *gopis* are bathing in the River Jumna, he hides their clothes in a tree and baits them from its upper branches when they come out of the water; they are keen to hide their nakedness but are unable to do so. In later scholasticism this scene is interpreted as illustrating the need for the devotee to abandon everything, and indeed every convention, to approach Lord Krishna. There are many other stories of this dalliance but one other that is frequently encountered concerns the 'the round dance of bliss', the *rasamandala*, the time when all the *gopis*, besotted with love for Krishna, run to the forest to join him in dancing. In the round dance that results each one believes that they alone are dancing with their beloved. So intoxicatingly magical is Krishna that he is able to replicate himself – either in their imaginations or literally – so that each of the *gopis* believes that she dances with him alone. This activity with all the *gopis* is, in a sense, but a prelude to the most profound and intimate of his relations, that with Radha. She is one of the *gopis*, but in the later, and particularly the Bengali, tradition she becomes his greatest favourite, despite his tendency to stray and cause her bitter unhappiness (never for too long, however, as this is Vrindavana where all is pure delight). In the Bengali theology of Krishna the two of them, together, are envisaged as a necessary part of the overall divinity.

As far as Bengal is concerned, the episodes of Krishna's life after he leaves Vrindavana are of less concern, and they can be quickly listed. Eventually, the day arrives when he returns to Mathura and after killing the various champions of Kamsa, he installs the rightful ruler on the throne of Mathura. He later withdraws to the city of Dwaraka, in western India, and marries Rukmini; Radha does not figure in this part of the story. The last substantial part of his myth concerns his involvement in the great epic narrative of India, the *Mahabharata*. He takes part in several episodes but makes his most famous appearance as the charioteer of the hero Arjuna on the eve of the battle of Kurukshetra. At this point he provides counsel to Arjuna, and this advice has its own separate and famous identity as the *Bhagavadgita* within the overall text of the *Mahabharata*. The *Bhagavadgita* is probably the single most influential of any text of Indian spirituality, especially on account of its teachings dealing with *dharma*, the requirement for each individual to follow his or her own ordained position in life. As far as the Bengali Krishna tradition is concerned, though, this part of the much larger *Mahabharata* – while known of and honoured – is less important than that which concerns the blissful sporting of Krishna with Radha in the eternal land of Vrindavana.

The history of Krishna devotion: the *Bhagavata Purana* and the *Gitagovinda*

Although both the *Mahabharata* and the later *Harivamsa* (early centuries AD) record some of the episodes listed above, the canonical work for the later Bengali view of Krishna's exploits is the early tenth-century text, the *Bhagavata Purana*, and in particular chapter 10. In the *Bhagavata Purana*, which appears to be of south Indian origin, many of the then new ideas concerning unconditional devotion to the divine, known by the Sanskrit term *bhakti*, are linked to the story of Krishna for the first time (incidentally, the notion of *bhakti* itself also appears to be of south Indian origin). The view of Krishna that emphasized his epic qualities, as delineated in the *Mahabharata* and the *Harivamsa*, recede in importance and are replaced by the qualities apparent in the tenth chapter of the *Bhagavata Purana* with its idyllic pastoral and erotic sensibilities. This in the later medieval period was viewed as the summation of all that was most profound in the theology of Krishna. However, the position of Radha, the *gopi* who eventually becomes the beloved of Krishna, in the *Bhagavata Purana* appears still to be mostly undifferentiated from the other *gopis*. Her moment of full realization comes later, although the 'prehistory' of her cult remains the subject of debate among scholars.

While many of the episodes of Krishna's life listed above appear throughout India in both scripture and sculpture during the medieval period under the influence of the *Bhagavata Purana*, the appearance of the Sanskrit poem, the *Gitagovinda*, marks the next important step in the development of the cult of Krishna in eastern India. The *Gitagovinda*, 'the Love Song of the Dark Lord', by the poet Jayadeva is a lyrical and erotic composition concerned with Krishna. While the poem is entirely the realization of the poet, some of the episodes draw on those that appear in the earlier *Bhagavata Purana*. It was composed in the second half of the twelfth century somewhere in eastern India; candidates for Jayadeva's place of birth are found in Orissa, in the Mithila district of Bihar and also in Bengal. In all these areas, as indeed elsewhere in India, the text has provided a rich vein of imagery for dancers and painters but, above all, for singers, as the poem is – as its name suggests – to be sung, and according to ragas specific to different parts of the poem. Even today parts of it are sung daily in the Jagannatha temple at Puri, where Jayadeva probably lived at the time of its composition.

The text describes the overtly erotic story of Krishna's sporting with the *gopis* in luscious and highly sensuous language, which hovers between the sacred and the profane by eschewing definition in a typically Indian way. This is noticeable, above all, with Radha, who now comes to the forefront of the narrative. The poem is arch-like in form with love-making between Krishna and Radha at both the beginning and the end. The central parts are taken up with Krishna's diversions with other *gopis*, Radha's despondency, Krishna's remorse and then the final reconciliation. The dramatic climax in the last section of the poem deals with the physical union of the two lovers, although much of the emotion preceding this is concerned with their separation, with jealousy and regret – on both sides – and their longing for eventual reunion deep in the forest in a bower on the edge of the River Jumna. Devotees have understood these emotions as a mirror of the longing of the soul for the lord, although they may not have been so intended and may be a later gloss. In eastern India this powerfully erotic text, which revels in imagery drawn from the world of the fecund and blossoming forest, provided fertile ground for the development of the cults that were to follow, based on the total abandonment of the self in a sensuous and charged love for Krishna. Typical are the following verses from the Sixth Song, where during their separation Radha fantasizes about her love-play with Krishna ('Friend' refers to an intermediary between the two lovers, while 'Kesi's sublime tormentor', mentioned in the refrain, refers to Krishna):

I shy from him when we meet; he coaxes me with flattering words,
I smile at him tenderly as he loosens the silken cloth on my hips.
　　Friend, bring Kesi's sublime tormentor to revel with me!
　　I've gone mad waiting for his fickle love to change.

I fall on the bed of tender ferns: he lies on my breasts forever.
I embrace him, kiss him; he clings to me drinking my lips.
　　Friend, bring Kesi's sublime tormentor to revel with me!
　　I've gone mad waiting for his fickle love to change.

(Miller, *Love Song of the Dark Lord*, p. 80)

From this time onwards there is no doubt that the individualized figure of Radha is the one who primarily engages the affections of Krishna.

Chaitanya and Shankaradeva

The specifically Bengali aspects of Krishna devotion were undoubtedly greatly influenced by the *Gitagovinda*, as well as by the poetry of other, later devotional writers such as Vidyapati and Chandidas (both fifteenth century). Even more important, though undoubtedly dependent on this earlier literary activity, were the life and teachings of the remarkable saint and ecstatic, Chaitanya (*c.*1486–1533). The story of Chaitanya is most authoritatively recorded in the early seventeenth-century text, the *Caitanyacaritamrita* of Krishnadas Kaviraj. From this and other hagiographical literature we learn that Chaitanya – often also known by the nickname Gauranga (literally, 'the golden-limbed') – was born in the town of Navadvip, north of present-day Calcutta. His father

Chaitanya in composite form as Rama (green-limbed and with bow), Krishna (blue-limbed and with flute) and Chaitanya (golden-limbed). Painting on paper from the Kalighat shrine in Calcutta, c.1890.

Jagannatha Misra was a brahmin, and the young child was named Visvambhara (Chaitanya, the name he is known by to posterity, was the name he took as a renunciant). As a child, he was taught in the schools of Navadvip, which were famous especially for Sanskrit and logic; the legends tell us that he excelled there and that he later set up his own school. He also married twice, on account of the early death of his first wife from snake bite.

The story tells that the all-important moment of change came upon him when he made a visit to the town of Gaya in Bihar. He had gone there to perform the death ceremonies, *shraddha*, for his father. While there, and in a way that we can no longer fathom from the legendary literature, he underwent a religious experience so profound that, when he returned home, he was an obsessed devotee of Krishna and soon gave up the life of a teacher and a householder; he was lost in devotion to Krishna. This new phase of his life was marked by unabashed and complete abandonment, most characteristically exemplified in the new form of devotion that he and his associates in Navadvip developed, the *sankirtan*. This was made up of a number of features based on congregational devotion. Essential were calling on the name of Krishna and singing of his love for Radha, and of hers for him. To these were added the playing of the drum, *khol*, and of the cymbals, *kartal*, and, as the emotion gathered intensity, wild devotional dancing, followed eventually by an uncontrolled procession through the streets. The passion engendered by this activity was intense, and Chaitanya is recorded as falling to the ground in divine delirium and entering trances in which he had visions of Krishna and Krishna's beloved, Radha. From now on *bhakti*, the unconditional devotion for and surrender to the godhead, became the all-encompassing purpose of his life.

This energetic and frenzied singing of hymns to Krishna and Radha is still today associated with Chaitanya and the movement that followed him; it became, in effect, devotional street-theatre. Recalling that these *kirtans* were sung by men and women and by members of different castes, and above all in Bengali, one scholar has tellingly said 'that he [Chaitanya] taught the Bangla language to speak the divine' (Kaviraj, *Literary Cultures in History*, p. 525).

The influence of Chaitanya on his followers was so great that even in his own lifetime he was regarded as an incarnation of Krishna or indeed in some mystical way as a combination, in one body, of both Krishna and Radha. He thus represented the ultimate, as he experienced not only the love of Krishna for Radha but also hers for him. Paintings from the Kalighat shrine in Calcutta show him in both this and (in nineteenth- and early twentieth-century versions) a further syncretic form (see illustration p. 49), where he is six armed and bearing the attributes of Rama (green arms and a bow), Krishna (blue arms and playing the flute) and the historical figure of Chaitanya (yellow arms and carrying the bag and staff of the mendicant).

In Navadvip he gathered around him a group of disciples, important among whom was Nityananda. He was, in a sense, seen as Chaitanya's brother and thus, in the same way that Chaitanya was considered to be Krishna, Nityananda was held to be an incarnation of Krishna's brother Balarama. In popular prints from the early lithographic presses of the late nineteenth cen-

Congregational devotion, or sankirtan.
In the centre Chaitanya (in red) and
Nityananda (in blue) are shown along with
other devotees in Navadvip. Lithograph,
Chore Bagan Art Studio, Calcutta, c.1895.

Print depicting Chaitanya on the left, with Krishna and Radha at the top in the arch, and Nityananda and Chaitanya on the right, with Balarama and Krishna at the top in the arch. Lithograph, Chore Bagan Art Studio, Calcutta, c.1895.

tury the two appear together flanked by their 'earlier' forms, Krishna and Balarama. It may have been through the influence of Nityananda (often colloquially known as Nitai) that ideas linked to the tantras, as well as caste inclusivity, became a stream of the new Bengali devotion to Krishna. This sub-school envisaged the physical body of the devotee as actually containing Krishna himself. The body was viewed as a microcosm of the cosmic, universal Krishna, a realization facilitated by rituals that included sexual union with a female devotee. In this sectarian view the male devotee could actually become Krishna, rather than merely being an attendant on Krishna, ever separate from but in the presence of the godhead. These ideas about microcosm and macrocosm surely draw on earlier tantric concepts that were current in both Buddhist and Hindu cults in eastern India in the twelfth and thirteenth centuries.

Although Chaitanya's period of wild devotionalism in Navadvip was intense, it was also short-lived, and he took the vow of a homeless renunciant at the age of twenty-four. For most of the rest of his life he lived in Puri in modern-day Orissa, not far from Bengal but nevertheless separate from it. Here he venerated the image of Krishna known as Jagannatha (literally, 'the Lord of the World') and regularly heard, and admired, Jayadeva's *Gitagovinda*. He travelled to other parts of India, touring extensively in the south where devotion to Krishna had a long history. He also went to Vrindavana in northern India, visiting and substantiating the actual places where it was believed Krishna had lived during his youth and where his *lila*, or divine play, was enacted. The emotional effect on the saint of experiencing the actual localities where Krishna had spent his glorious and unfettered youth, dancing and playing with the *gopis* on the banks of the River Jumna, was almost completely overwhelming for him. His later years in Puri passed mildly especially in comparison to his early years, although throughout his life he received pilgrims from Bengal and experienced ecstatic visions of Radha and Krishna. His influence on Bengali life right up to the present day has been immense.

The way of *bhakti*, of unquestioning love for the deity, found its focus in Bengal in the notion of Krishna as the young, handsome lover of Radha, the cowgirl, whose life – like that of the devotee – was one of constant longing for the presence of her lord Krishna. Chaitanya specifically developed the idea of *viraha bhakti*, the *bhakti* of separation. Just as Radha spent most of the time longing to be reunited with Krishna, so in Chaitanya's system does the devotee. There thus grew up an equivalence between the devotee and Radha; both had their attention forever focused on Krishna. From the point of view of the devotee the time when the beloved is absent is the most testing. This is when trust is most important and the idea of the devotee emulating Radha, longing to be with Krishna but not able to, became in Bengal the acme of all types of devotion. Those who honoured Krishna were encouraged to dwell on the pains of sorrow and the joy of eventual (re)union with the lord. Allied to this is the story about the inconstancy of Krishna (providing further challenges to test the courage and steadfastness of the devotee). The legend tells how Krishna and Radha have a lover's tiff and as a result are temporarily estranged. Radha then frets over Krishna's absence and meanwhile Krishna spends the night away from his beloved. When they meet again, they are both remorseful but neither is certain how to return to their old relationship. Radha turns away while Krishna tries to approach, a scene that is frequently depicted (see illustration overleaf). Sometimes her friends try to patch up their differences and other times he cajoles and entreats her, but eventually, of course, she accepts him back, despite the evidence on his handsome blue body of last night's love-play with someone other than herself.

In nearby Assam, just to the north of Bengal, devotion to Krishna is associated with the equally charismatic and saintly figure of Shankaradeva (died 1568). Shankaradeva also went on pilgrimage, though mostly to sites in northern India. A miraculous story is told of how the *Bhagavata Purana* came to be the basis of the devotional cult that he founded. A brahmin pundit, Jagdish Misra, came to Puri to read the *Bhagavata Purana* to the image of Lord

Krishna approaching Radha. Painted wooden book cover (inner face), Bengal; the manuscript originally associated with this book cover was dated 1647 and the painting is likely to be of the same date.

Jagannatha in the great temple (Jagannatha is the deity of Puri who is regarded as a form of Krishna). While there, he had a dream in which the deity told him to take a copy of the text to Assam, where he was to find Shankaradeva and read it to him, too. This Jagdish Misra did, reading all twelve books to the saint. The contents of the text had such a profound effect on Shankaradeva that from that time onwards he made this text concerned with devotion to Krishna the basis of all his teachings. One feature of this *bhakti* cult that was different to that propounded by Chaitanya was that it was practised almost entirely without images. The most important elements of the cult became congregational singing of the god's praises and the calling on his and Radha's names by devotees in prayer-halls, or *namghars*.

A striking exception to the rule of worship without images is seen in the outstanding woven-silk textiles that use themes from the Krishna legend as the basis for their decoration. These were made in Assam for ritual use in the Krishna cult in the sixteenth and seventeenth centuries. In one register after another they show scenes from Krishna's life in Vrindavana, along with other mythological scenes. The Krishna stories illustrated include the defeat of the snake-king Kaliya and of the crane-demon Bakasura sent by the evil King of Mathura, Kamsa, to assassinate Krishna. Bakasura triumphantly swallows up the divine hero only to find him unbearably hot. He consequently has to vomit him out or risk being burnt to death, and Krishna then swiftly kills him. All these episodes are part of Krishna's *lila*, his play, for nothing can truly alter or interrupt his eternally graceful and delightful existence – all of which is so captivatingly different from the material world from which his devotees long to escape.

Detail from a large silk textile (12 metres/39 feet long) depicting scenes from the story of Krishna, including the defeat of the crane-demon, Bakasura. Woven silk textile, Assam, late 17th century.

Krishna and his dalliance

In eastern India Krishna is most commonly depicted in painting and in sculpture as the young shepherd-god standing with one leg crossed over the other and his hands in the position of playing the flute. The stories tell of the enchanting effect of Krishna's flute music, as it floats in from the jungle to the settled houses of the cowherds' village of Vrindavana. It sends the *gopis*, above all Radha, into paroxysms of longing and desire (the phallic symbolism of the flute has been noted by scholars). Radha is so distraught at the promise evoked by the sound of the flute that she forgets what she is supposed to be doing – she puts her necklace around her waist, she puts her earrings on her toes and her armbands on her legs. Other *gopis* similarly leave the pot of food being prepared for the family on the fire, abandon the milking of the cows half-done or interrupt the application of eye make-up. They all run to the forest at the command of Krishna's flute. At this point Radha, just like the devotee when he hears the call, must abandon the constancies of settled family life and run off to join with the playful god in his *lila*. In most versions of the story she is married to another of the cowherds, Ayana, and her relationship with Krishna is therefore illicit and full of risk. The commitment that she shows is known as *parakiya* and is taken as the epitome of devotion to the god because of its difficulty.

The emotions engendered by these ideas are frequently enacted in dance, singing, storytelling and above all in devotional poetry, as well as being shown in painting and in architectural decoration, but they are also those into which the devotee is called upon to enter. This state of mind is unquestionably encouraged through the reading, declaiming and ecstatic singing of the sensuous poetry centred on Krishna. As the young flute-playing deity, two-armed in human form and the quintessence of rapture, Krishna is approachable and understandable to his devotees and is thus most often depicted in this way in Bengal sculpture of recent centuries. In other popular images he is shown with Radha, sometimes merged as one figure and thus implying the presence of Chaitanya, or standing separately but embracing and located within the sacred syllable, 'Om'. Frequently, they are portrayed standing beneath the flowering tree, the *kadamba*, with its large white flowers. As the cult of Krishna developed in Bengal, the position of Radha became more and more important, perhaps drawing on the ancient tradition in Bengal of tantrism, which emphasized the power and imminence of the female force and thus provided a pattern into which the personality of Radha could be fitted. Mythologically, all of this was located in the forests around Vrindavana on the banks of the Jumna but pictured as being firmly planted in Bengal, for this is, of course, the only landscape known to the majority of the Bengali devotees of Krishna. Indeed, there is evidence at the temple town of Bishnupur, in south-western Bengal, that there was a deliberate attempt to replicate locally the divine landscape of Vrindavana. The sweet and luscious dream of Vrindavana remains an extremely intoxicating vision in the Bengali cult of Krishna.

Among the stories of Krishna's *lila*, another favourite in Bengal tells how he ferried the *gopis* across the river, entertaining them delightfully with his flute.

This narrative conforms to eastern Indian notions of what is utterly desirable in terms of luxurious relaxation. In the early twentieth century the poet Rabindranath Tagore wrote in a letter that he was worried about his rebirth – how tiresome it would be if he was reborn in Europe and was thus not able to lie around in a boat on the water, relaxing and enjoying the river breeze. To be ferried across the water by a boatman, who doubtless also entertained with a song, was a delicious vision to conjure up in the days before air conditioning.

Boats of many types are known throughout the delta country; they are the best way to get around where roads are few and constantly under threat from inundation, and in the prints and paintings of this scene from the Krishna *lila* a range of them are depicted. In the illustration below, Krishna and the *gopis* are shown making the crossing in a *murpankhi*, or vessel with a peacock prow. Radha is seated apart in a small, classically inspired cabin, for all the world as if in an eighteenth-century English garden gazebo; from the top of the cabin a pennant gaily flutters. Krishna stands in the stern, flute in one hand and steering oar in the other. He is the helmsman steering a way, not only across the river but also through the complexities of phenomenal existence. His dark skin – appropriate for a forest deity – is deliberately contrasted with the fair-

Krishna ferrying the gopis *across the river. The river is the Jumna in the story yet to the viewer the setting is unequivocally Bengali. Metal-cut print probably produced in Battala, north Calcutta, in the early 19th century.*

57

ness of the *gopis* who face him in adoring admiration; this trip across the river is yet another opportunity for flirting and erotic indulgence. Those of the *gopis* who stand carry flat baskets on their heads on which are depicted small vessels containing milk or a dairy preparation (they are, after all, keepers of cow herds). Is it fanciful to imagine that they are carrying that most delicious of all Bengali sweets, *misti-doi* (sweetened rich yoghurt)? The stock comic character in the Bengali Krishna *lila*, the widow Barai-buri, berates Krishna with upraised hand and frowning visage, and acts as a foil to the god. This type of boat with its peacock imagery is particularly appropriate for Krishna, as the gaudy, strutting forest bird is closely associated with him: its call from the forest mimics the sound of his flute inviting the *gopis*, and its beautiful tail-feathers are used to decorate his crown, as can be seen in this print.

The child Krishna

While the stories of Krishna's dalliance in the groves of Vrindavana with the *gopis* and with Radha are the best known and loved in Bengal, others deal with his childhood. Krishna as the focus for the unconditional love given without thought by a mother to a child has been popular in Bengal as a metaphor for the love that a devotee ideally expresses for the divine. Small sculptures of the crawling child Krishna often appear on the domestic altars of devotees. In popular prints he is frequently shown naughtily stealing butter, and being gently reprimanded, and in the texts we also read the famous story of how he eats dirt from the ground. The legend tells that, when he was scolded for this by his stepmother, he disingenuously opens his mouth and reveals, not the grubby earth he has stuffed in there as any child might, but the entire universe. She unwittingly experiences an epiphany, as all that exists in the whole cosmos is contained within the divine child. An unusual depiction of this early part of his life is shown in the Bengali oil painting opposite. Here, in front of a throne, the child Krishna is pictured along with ritual objects typically used in puja in Bengal including a copper water pourer, conch shell and bell. Most intriguing, however, is that what at first glance appears to be an empty throne behind the child is probably not intended as such. The circular black object that is garlanded and propped up on the seat of the throne is probably a *salagram*, an ammonite fossil. These circular stones, which occur in, and are collected from, the gorge of the Kali Gandaki river in western Nepal, are believed in India to be naturally occurring forms of the god Vishnu and, by extension, of Krishna, who for his devotees is not just the eighth incarnation of Vishnu but the supreme deity above all others. Thus, on the altars of many Bengali families the *salagram* has pride of place at puja, rather than a metal or stone image. This seems to be in contradistinction to what is found in temples, where a metal image is more usual.

The child Krishna with, behind, the enthroned salagram *(ammonite fossil form of Vishnu/Krishna). Oil painting on canvas, Bengal, c.1890.*

Conclusion

The distinctive qualities of Krishna's story in Bengal are sweet. The pan-Indian myths, which are already very dense, are highlighted here through emphasis on the erotic, the pleasurable, the verdant and the uncomplicated. These layers have been added in eastern India through the vision of saints and poets such as Chaitanya and Jayadeva. In this view Krishna allows his devotees to enjoy a world that is accessible and delightful. His myth is not elaborated with paradox like that of Mother Kali, and there is no difficult resolution of apparent opposites. All that Krishna asks in Bengal is for unencumbered devotion, and in return he gives pleasure.

Manasa, Kamalekamini, Gazi and Rama

In this chapter three stories local to eastern India are presented, although one of these, the one that goes by the generic name of Gazi, is only incompletely presented, as it is not fully understood. However, notable among all three are substantial maritime and mercantile elements, reminding us that the delta was always an area with commercial links beyond the immediate shores of Bengal. The last of the four, that of Rama, has a pan-Indian currency but is included here, as it demonstrates certain features that can be considered specific to Bengal.

The story of the snake-goddess Manasa

Throughout the Indian subcontinent the worship of snake deities has an ancient history. Some of the very earliest-surviving sculptures, from the Buddhist period, indicate the importance of the king of the snakes, the *nagaraja*; the earliest of these date to the late centuries BC. In eastern India the evidence will not allow us to go back that far, but already in the Pala period (eighth to twelfth centuries AD) the local variant of this widely spread cult is apparent. Here, the deity is female and is known as Manasa. The stories described below may well go back to these medieval times, but we cannot be certain, as the literature that records Manasa's myth appears in oral form somewhat later, perhaps only in the fifteenth century, and then is not written down until several centuries after that.

Manasa, whose remit is the realm of snakes and serpents and who is depicted garlanded with or accompanied by them, is primarily a deity of eastern India. Her festival is held in the summer months, the time of the monsoon, when snakes are flushed up out of the ground by the rains. She can be represented in bodily form, attended by or holding snakes, or as a full-bodied pot decorated with snakes or sometimes with the top part of the vessel closed in and modelled in the shape of the goddess's face. The link between this deity and pots appears also in her story. In the subcontinent her legend has been recorded in the modern states of Bihar, Orissa, West Bengal, Assam and Tripura (all in

Bronze sculpture of the goddess Manasa
(the eyes are inlaid with silver). Eastern India,
probably Bengal, early Pala period, c. AD 750.

India) and in Bangladesh. Her personality is both benign (she protects from snakes) and malevolent (she inflicts the deadly snake bite); she is morally ambiguous, and this element continues today, as will be evident in the account detailed below. Her story is first recorded in the various *Manasakavya* texts, which consist of poetry – *kavya* – concerning the goddess Manasa; the most famous is probably one composed by the late fifteenth-century poet Vipradas.

These poems belong to the large general body of Bengali literature known as *Mangalkavya*. Originally transmitted orally, they dealt for the most part with tales of the deities of Bengal, such as Manasa, who have a local, eastern Indian existence, rather than a pan-Indian one. The narratives in the *Mangalkavya* frequently involve the life stories of the devotees of these gods and the way in which the divine presence is manifested. Another common theme in this literature is the struggle between the gods – often the smaller gods of the local tradition – for the attention of devotees. This is a prominent feature of the Manasa story and presumably reflects a time of change and uncertainty in religious matters in the late medieval/early modern period, when Islam (both Sufi and orthodox) and the *bhakti* cults centred on Krishna were competing with local cults (such as that of Manasa), as well as with the earlier-established cults of the great deities Shiva and Vishnu. In a way that is unique to Bengal these religious strands often crossed over and were incorporated into each other.

The story of her birth makes Manasa a child of Shiva. Given that male deity's complicated sex life, it is not surprising that she was born through the ejaculation of his sperm onto a lotus leaf growing in a pond. From here it travelled down to the kingdom of the snakes, Patala, deep below the waters. The wife of Vasuki, the king of the snakes, made a model of a beautiful girl, which was brought to life by the touch of Shiva's sperm. This was Manasa, and from that time onwards she has been associated with ponds and tanks, and with the lotus plant, all constants in the life of the watery country of Bengal. The best-remembered tale of Manasa, wonderfully translated by the great scholar of Bengali literature, Edward Dimock, in *The Thief of Love* (1963) is one of the competition stories mentioned above and revolves around the goddess being eventually, though grudgingly, accepted as a fit focus for devotion.

Based on Dimock, the narrative goes as follows. There existed a devotee of Shiva called Chando who lived in the city of Champakanagara. He was a wealthy and famous merchant, trading widely and having many ships at his command. However, although he honoured Shiva, he refused to revere Manasa and indeed abused the golden pots on her altar. Thus the stage was set for him to be humbled and for the cult of the snake goddess to be eventually brought into the fold of the great gods. Powerful Manasa, angered by Chando's unwillingness to worship her, caused a cataclysmic storm to wreck his cargo fleet while on a trading venture. The storm also killed his six sons and only narrowly missed killing him. He is left to wander far and wide, only eventually finding his way home, having lost everything but still determined in his opposition to the goddess. Meanwhile, back in Champakanagara his wife Sanaka has given birth to their seventh son Lakhindar. Today, it is the story of this son and his virtuous wife Behula, a model of wifely virtue held up as an ideal for all young

Part of a scroll-painting depicting the story of the goddess Manasa. Scrolls such as this are still occasionally used to accompany recitations of the story of the goddess. Painting by Gurupada Chitrakar, West Bengal, early 21st century.

Bengali women, that is most remembered and frequently used in the painted scrolls of the itinerant storytellers. At the same time as Lakhindar's birth Behula is born into another merchant family and she grows up – fortunately – with due respect for the snake goddess. When the time comes, and after much examining of horoscopes, the two are married in magnificent style and go to spend their first night on the Saitali mountain in a specially constructed iron house, protected from the evil that Chando, quite correctly, surmises will be directed by Manasa towards them as they are his son and daughter-in-law. Chando has had this iron house built by Vishvakarma, the architect of the gods, but, unknown to him, Vishvakarma has been bribed by Manasa to leave a small hole in the structure through which one of her deadly snakes can gain access to the newly-wed couple; the immorality of human life is mirrored all too clearly by immorality in the heavens!

During the dead hours of the night, as her husband sleeps, Behula attacks three of the venomous messengers sent by Manasa to kill her husband, but finally she succumbs to sleep. On awakening she finds to her horror that her husband has, despite her earlier vigil, been bitten by a snake and died. The ensuing tumult following his death – and this on their very wedding night as well – can be imagined. Also the position of Behula herself becomes very difficult as the lot of a young Bengali widow in the past was far from enviable. However, Behula is no ordinary girl and, calling on the name of Manasa, she decides not to consign the body of her dead husband to the flames, as would be normal, but to carry him on the waters of the river until, through her enduring love for him, she can bring him back to life. Against all the remonstrations of her husband's family, she sets out on a raft made of bamboo, cradling the body of her dead husband in her lap.

Down the river she floats and after some time is accompanied by an entourage of crocodiles and fish all able to smell the dead body that she carries slowly decaying in her lap. The rotting flesh, in which flies and worms crawl and breed, causes great excitement among the beasts of land and water, who smell its overpowering stench. Indeed, at one point one of the greatest of the fish manages to snatch at and eat one of Lakhindar's knees. After this Behula gathers up his remaining bones and hides them in her sari. Fighting off the animals, as well as the attentions of lascivious men on the river banks, Behula floats on down the river, with her raft disintegrating beneath her and the wild animals circling ever closer, eager to be in on the kill when the final moment comes.

At this moment of apparent and ultimate disaster, Behula – still confident in the power of Manasa – comes upon the washerwoman of the gods, carrying out her duties on the riverbank; she is none other than the handmaiden of Manasa, Neto. Behula persuades Neto to let her help with the washing and the gods are so pleased with the result that they call Behula into their company. Here Behula dances for them, cradling her dead husband's bones in her dress. They are so delighted with her performance, especially the old roué Shiva, that he grants Behula a favour. She, of course, asks for the life of her husband to be restored, and after yet further trials Behula is granted her wish by Manasa herself, in front of all the other gods. A short delay in the fulfilment of this wish is caused by the loss of the kneecap that the great fish had swallowed, and it is not until the fish has been caught, its stomach opened and the bone recovered that Lakhindar's beautiful and shining body can once more be re-assembled by Manasa herself. Behula, in her turn, agrees to persuade her father-in-law to honour the name and cult of the snake goddess. Manasa is by now so enchanted by the devotion of Behula that she readily grants her further favours. She restores to life the six sons who were drowned, as well as the cargo ships (now magically multiplied from seven to fourteen). This grand assembly eventually makes its way back to Champakanagara, where after yet further adventures the chief characters are reunited with Chando and Sanaka. Chando finally, though even at this point grudgingly, acknowledges Manasa (it is said that he made his first offering to her with his left hand, the unclean hand), and all live 'happily ever after'.

This story is fascinating not only on account of its great narrative qualities but also because it throws up some interesting questions. Why, for instance, does Shiva not intervene earlier on in the proceedings; he is, after all, the father of Manasa, and Chando is his unswerving devotee? Chando has a Job-like quality, enduring untold miseries, holding unswervingly to his devotion, and yet is not supported by Shiva. There is a moral ambiguity that is slightly unnerving. In this scenario Shiva's actions seem a little churlish, although this is probably to be explained by the fact of Manasa's comparatively late inclusion within the panoply of the great gods. Although in the story she is indeed the daughter of Shiva, this relationship probably reflects the forcing of her non-orthodox cult into the arena of what was then to become orthodox. Also, we are left to ask, why is Manasa so ungracious and demanding? The deities behave just like jealous humans; her behaviour is far from admirable and not what one would expect of a goddess. Interestingly, the story also points up the importance of the river system (in the full recitations there are long descriptions of the different branches of the great river down which Behula's raft floats) and its animal life. Further, the first part dealing with Chando's mercantile activity goes into detail about the products that are being traded and the vessels that are used; the importance of maritime trade appears very significant. Finally, there is an interesting echo of the story of Savitri from the *Mahabharata*, where a devout wife also manages to outwit the god of death, Yama, and bring her dead husband back to life.

The story of Kamalekamini

The narrative of Kamalekamini ('the Lady on the Lotus') derives from the same tradition and shares several of the same features of the Manasa story. As in the Manasa tale, it revolves around a merchant who honours Shiva and is disrespectful towards the newcomer deity, in this instance the goddess Chandi rather than Manasa. This goddess, again like Manasa, is worshipped in the form of a golden water pot and thus, by implication, has a general overview of fertility and prosperity. Her story is also narrated in the *Mangalkavya* literature, the versions of the tales about local deities written in the local Bengali tongue. Both Chandi and Manasa come from this same eastern Indian narrative background. The Chandi story survives in the text of the sixteenth-century *Chandimangala-kavya* associated with the name of Mukundaram Chakravarty. We also learn more of the rich merchant's trade this time – his mercantile activity takes him all the way to Sri Lanka, underlining the fact that the delta country thrived on its long-distance maritime trade.

A merchant named Dhanapati, who lived in the city of Ujani, had two wives, Lahana and Khullana. Khullana, the second and thus more vulnerable wife, was a devotee of Chandi and several stories are told about the protection given her by the goddess. On one occasion, prior to his departure for Sri Lanka with a fleet of twelve boats, Dhanapati discovers her devotion to the goddess and in a temper kicks over the sacred water pots that are Chandi's image (a very similar episode appears in the story of Manasa when the destitute merchant Chando is wandering back home after the shipwreck). Not surprisingly, Chandi

The goddess Kamalekamini appearing to Shrimanta. The metal plate for the print has broken at both upper right and lower left, and in the latter case it has been mended with two screws whose imprint appears in the image. Hand-coloured metal-cut print probably produced at Bat-tala, north Calcutta, early 19th century.

takes against Dhanapati and has him marked out for attention. Meanwhile, Dhanapati goes off on a long trade voyage to Sri Lanka and, while on the high seas, has a vision of a goddess seated on a lotus. In this vision, extraordinarily, the goddess both devours and then vomits up elephants. On arrival in Sri Lanka, the merchant visits King Salban with whom he is trading, and tells him the story of 'the Lady on the Lotus'. Astonished, the king commands to be shown this and the merchant agrees, having been threatened with a long spell in prison if he fails. Given the opposition of the goddess, he does fail and is consequently thrown into jail.

Meanwhile, back in Bengal, Khullana, the second wife and devotee of Chandi, gives birth to a fine son, Shrimanta, through the grace of the goddess. After many years, and because of the taunts of his guru for not apparently having a father, Shrimanta sets out for Sri Lanka to find Dhanapati. In a further link with the Manasa story, due to Khullana's supplication, the goddess Chandi engages the divine mastercraftsman, Vishvakarma, to build the boats to transport Shrimanta's party (Vishvakarma built the iron house on Mount Saitali for the merchant Chando in the Manasa tale). On his way to Sri Lanka Shrimanta, just like his father, has a vision of the goddess in the middle of the sea, apparently seated on a lotus and surrounded by many others; in her lap is an elephant, and she also swallows and belches out elephants (see opposite). The boat in which Shrimanta is travelling is of the distinctive Bengali type with a peacock prow and an elephant stern known in the delta country as a *mur-pankhi* (see p. 57 for an example in the Krishna legend). On the prow is a cabin with Georgian-style windows, while on top, seated on a European chair, Shrimanta is pointing to the appearance of the deity, visible to him alone, in the water beyond. The sky all around this unearthly scene is filled with butterflies. The print, with its stencilled but hand-painted decoration, is clearly one of many on account of the crack in the plate that can be seen replicated at top right. The story, fortunately, has a happy ending, for Shrimanta is a devotee of Chandi, and when he, like his father, tells the King of Sri Lanka about his vision and is required to substantiate it, he can. As a reward for this feat, his father is restored to him along with his cargo, and he gains the daughter of the Sri Lankan king, Sushila, as his wife.

Like the Manasa tale, this narrative records the way in which a non-orthodox deity becomes recognized as being of equal status to the great, pan-Indian gods. Here Chandi takes on the features of Lakshmi, the goddess of plenty who is also associated with elephants and is invariably depicted seated on a lotus.

শ্রীনবকৃষ্ণ সা. গোবাবাজার শ্রীশ্রীকমলেকামিনী   শ্রীমন্তেবকমলিনীদর্শন   শ্রীগুপীচরন স্বর্ণকাবের ঘোদিত সা. কোন্নলেগোলা

The Gazi scroll and its narrative

This story is different from the previous two in that, while we can guess the type involved, we only have a pictorial rather than a written or aural record of it. It is preserved in an astonishing scroll of the type used in Bengal for story-telling, as described on p. 22. This scroll is more than 13 metres (42 feet) in length and has fifty-four different registers of narrative. It is one of the great documents of Indian folk art. It tells the story of at least two Muslim saints, *pirs*, although the precise details are not apparent today. We can identify the *pir* in the painted scenes on account of his beard and above all his dress: he wears a *lungi* (single piece of cloth like a sarong) or sometimes trousers, and a cap, but never a dhoti. Further, his charismatic character is clearly indicated by the fact that people bow down before him, he waves a wand of peacock feathers and he has power over animals: a cow miraculously lactates when he touches its nostrils (see illustration p. 72); he charms the greatest and most feared denizen of the Bengal jungle, the tiger, to be his mount (see illustration overleaf); and cobras are at his beck and call – he even carries one as his staff.

67

*This figure, riding a tiger and carrying
a serpent-staff, is probably the Muslim
saint Gazi Pir. Register from the
painted Gazi scroll, Bengal, c.1800.*

The Muslim, though specifically Bengali Muslim, context of these holy men is also indicated by the depictions of Muslim shrines in the scroll – they are constructed in Bengali-hut style with down-curving thatch roofs, but there seems no doubt that they are meant to represent Islamic holy places. No images are seen in these shrines, the centre usually being taken up by a garlanded and censed tomb, illumined by lamps. Elsewhere, a fantastic and composite winged animal, with a human head (crowned), peacock's tail-feathers and a body that is part tiger, part camel, is perhaps meant to be a *buraq* – the mount of the Prophet. But this extraordinary beast appears to be carrying a catafalque with two turbans on it, so if it is indeed the *buraq* of tradition, it is in a different context to that of orthodox Islam. The Muslim element is further emphasized in another register where a naked Sufi is shown circumcized.

The tomb of a Muslim saint, attended by a devotee. Hanging above the tomb is a cloth, apparently made up of scraps of different-coloured textile sewn together. Such a cloth is given by a senior Sufi to his disciple as a mark of continuity of teaching. Register from the painted Gazi scroll, Bengal, c.1800.

The composite figure is perhaps meant to be Chaitanya (Krishna beyond and Radha near) or maybe the joint Vishnu and Shiva deity, Harihara (Krishna/Vishnu beyond and Shiva near). Register from the painted Gazi scroll, Bengal, c.1800.

However, it is important to record that Hindus also appear scattered throughout the narrative, reflecting the historically mixed and interpenetrated nature of Bengal society, especially in the countryside. At one point we see a blue-coloured male figure accompanied by a female, who are presumably Radha and Krishna in the mystically joined form popularized by Chaitanya (see pp. 49–53). This reminds us that in the early modern period Bengali authors, writing of figures such as the holy men seen in this scroll-painting, have suggested that the gods of the *Puranas*, above all Krishna, and the god of the Qur'an are one and the same and should thus receive the equal homage of the people. This is the same philosophical ground as is still occupied by the Bauls, the itinerant singers known for their desire to reveal the 'man of the heart'. Famously, the Bauls try to go beyond the sectarian divide of Muslim or Hindu in their understanding of the divine.

All these clues suggest that the narrative we are dealing with concerns one of the redoubtable saints who brought Islam to the remoter parts of Bengal, particularly the Sunderbans, the densely forested and watery region of the Ganges delta. Here legends have been recorded of a *pir*, sometimes called Gazi, although this seems to be no more than a generic name for 'warrior-saint' or similar. This *pir* not only brought the new faith to the virgin forest but also settled new converts in these remote areas, cutting down the impenetrable jungle and taming the wild animals, above all the tiger. Still today this battle between man, the animal world and the fruitful – as well as devastating – river continues. This is a theme that the Bengali author, Amitav Ghosh, has so powerfully evoked in his novel *The Hungry Tide* (London, 2004). Identifying all the scenes in this extravagantly lengthy tale, as depicted in the scroll, is also difficult because of the way in which some episodes about the *pir* – especially his connection with tigers – are duplicated in the stories of other, Hindu saints or demi-gods. Satya Pir (also known as Satya Narayan, Narayan being a name for Vishnu) is one such example.

Another constant of this scroll is the presence of the water, either the sea or the tributary rivers of the great delta, which geographically dominate the area of undivided Bengal. Sea-going ships, as well as boats suitable for the inland waterways of the Ganges–Brahmaputra system, are frequently and knowledgeably illustrated. This suggests a mercantile and riverine background to the narrative further emphasized by the many depictions of fish and other aquatic creatures in the painted registers, including, impressively, a crocodile. The mercantile element, also found in the two stories presented above, has been noted by Dineshchandra Sen, the well-known scholar of the oral literature of Bengal, in his pioneering volume *The Folk Literature of Bengal*, published in 1920. He specifically linked the maritime elements to a

A river crocodile, perhaps meant to represent the vehicle of the goddess of the Ganges. Register from the painted Gazi scroll, Bengal, c.1800.

much earlier – perhaps even a Buddhist stratum – of the folk literature of eastern India.

Since this giant scroll of the story of Gazi was first published in 1989, one series of scenes has, however, begun to be more understandable as a specific narrative. This is the part that can now perhaps be associated with a different saint – not Gazi Pir – but the saint known as Manik Pir. Here the work of Dineshchandra Sen is again important, and interestingly he begins the relevant section (p. 113) thus: 'Another saint who has also been deified by the Hindus and the Mahomedans alike, second only to Satya Pir in popular esteem – whose achievements and deeds have been extolled in many rural legends of Bengal – is Manik Pir, a Mahomedan Fakir.' He then goes on to tell the story of Manik Pir, much of which can be identified in the scroll, such as the scene when the young fakir is bound and thrown into a wooden box, which is then set alight. Manik also has connections with the cow-herding communities and specifically with the brothers Kinu and Kanu who lived successfully as sellers of dairy products. One day the *pir* solicited alms at the house but was abused by the old mother of the two brothers. When upbraided by the holy man, she tauntingly told him that he could have any amount of milk from one cow that she indicated. She knew that it was barren, but miraculously the *pir* caused it to produce milk by touching its nipples. Could this scene be the one in the scroll where the *pir* touches the nostrils of the cow and causes it to lactate (illustrated below)? The feud between the old woman and the *pir* continued, and to avenge himself, he has a cobra bite one of the two brothers, who consequently falls down dead. Later, when the family is still not united in devotion to the *pir*, he causes all their cattle and property to be destroyed in a fire. These scenes are all found in the scroll. Unfortunately, the story as recorded by Sen is not in quite the same order as shown in the scroll; also, this section of narrative is clearly only a small part of the total, which includes magnificent views of palace interiors and heroes riding on horseback, among much else.

The saint, probably Manik Pir, causing the barren cow to give milk. He is depicted wearing the distinctive robe of the Sufi, made up of multi-coloured scraps of cloth. Tucked beneath his arms he carries manuscripts. Register from the painted Gazi scroll, Bengal, c.1800.

The final register in a storytelling scroll-painting of the Ramayana *showing Rama and Sita enthroned with a parasol over their heads. This and the yak-tail whisk held by the figure in front of Rama are symbols of royalty. The quintessential devotee, Hanuman, stands at the far left. Bengal, c.1850.*

The story of Rama

The legend of Rama forms the basis of the great Indian epic, the *Ramayana*. This story is known throughout India and has very many regional variants and a huge number of individual parts. The basic thread of the narrative, which has an inordinate number of sub-plots, diversions and digressions, tells of King Rama, his exile to the forest, his triumph over demons, the capture of his wife Sita by the demon Ravana who lives in far-off Lanka, and then – after many adventures, not least with the monkey general and hero, Hanuman – the final defeat of Ravana. Following this, Rama and Sita are reunited and they return to the city of Ayodhya to their rightful rule.

It is unknown when the Sanskrit *Ramayana*, associated with the name of Valmiki, first became established in eastern India. The fifteenth-century poet Krittivasa is credited with the first presentation of it in Bengali language. This was not a word-for-word translation, and it also places the action very much within the Bengal cultural milieu. This repackaging of the epic took place some time in the fifteenth century, but Krittivasa's version has continued to be changed and added to ever since, with the result that it is no longer at all clear

73

Public recitation of the Ramayana *in the house of a wealthy man. Lithograph from Balthazar Solvyns,* Les Hindous, *vol. I, Paris, 1808.*

what Krittivasa first wrote. Explaining this, in part, is the fact that the legend of Rama has mostly been enjoyed in Bengal through oral transmission. In the cities recitations of the *Ramayana* episodes were given by professional reciters as part of a wealthy person's good works. In the countryside the stories were often told by itinerant storytellers using picture scrolls, as noted earlier; these narrators, still occasionally seen today, are known as *patuas* and have a distinctively high-pitched declamation called *patua-sangit*. Several examples of *Ramayana*-based scrolls survive. In the last two centuries these orally transmitted versions have run concurrently with printed editions of Krittivasa's *Ramayana* (from 1802) and with translations into English (from 1806).

One particular sequence has a specifically Bengali slant to it and this – not surprisingly – appears in the scroll-paintings. It provides a link between Rama and the goddess Durga, with her annual worship in the autumn (see pp. 28–37). In the story the evil Ravana is remembered as a devotee of Shiva and Durga. Every year he honoured her at a spring festival, and indeed Ravana, so the story goes, taught the Bengalis to worship her first in the spring. However, in order to finally defeat Ravana, Rama had to invoke Durga as the goddess of battle and, because it was not spring at the time, he was forced to approach her in the autumn. Before his final engagement with Ravana he made an out-of-season Puja to Durga and was horrified to discover that the requisite number of lotus blossoms for the Puja was not available; he was one short of the necessary and auspicious 108 (the goddess had actually hidden one of them to test him). He thus prepared to offer up one of his own eyes to replace the missing offering and is frequently depicted at this climatic moment, turning his bow and arrow on himself to gouge out an eye. Fortunately, the arrival of the goddess at this point ensured that this was not required. By such an indication of devotion he was able to secure the support of Durga and defeat Ravana. This episode, which is so popular in eastern India, is of the same type as those found in both the Manasa and the Chandi stories narrated above, where the devotee is tested, almost to the point of death.

The tale continues and the final outcome is given a specifically eastern Indian, *bhakti* type of finale. To assure the defeat of Ravana, Rama had to request Ravana to perform the Puja to Durga. As such a request cannot be denied by a brahmin, Ravana – who is represented here as the perfect brahmin – was forced to perform it. Further, as a part of the Puja and especially one for the goddess of battle, Rama built in the destruction of Ravana. Thus, by performing it, Ravana was signing his own death warrant. Fortunately, however – and here comes the *bhakti* element – by being killed by Rama, Ravana achieved further merit, as Rama is none other than Lord Vishnu incarnate on earth. From this time onwards the annual Durga Puja has taken place in the autumn and not in the spring, and this is the story told to explain it.

Episodes from the Ramayana: *Rama in his forest exile fighting a demon (above); Rishyashringa and the rishis reading the fire omens (centre); and the marriage of Rama, Lakshmana and their two brothers (below). Unusually, the episodes are not shown in the logical narrative order. Three of eight registers from a storytelling scroll, Bengal, early 19th century.*

Conclusion

The narratives in this chapter are closely related to the ancient traditions of professional storytelling in Bengal. Storytelling devices such as scrolls, recitation, songs and dance are all linked to these examples. They are also connected to other methods of encoding story that are distinctively eastern Indian, such as *alpana* (the auspicious designs made with rice paste on the house floor) and *brata* (the domestic rituals conducted by women for the provision of family health and wealth). These in their turn are also linked to the visual vocabulary of the *kantha*, the embroidered quilts that were such a feature of Bengali village life right up into living memory and can be 'read' to provide the stories located within them.

The appearance of these narratives is also part of the history of Bengali as a language, as it was used for the dissemination of this previously orally transmitted literature, first in manuscript and then eventually in published form. Further, all of these stories are, of course, only presented here in very much reduced form and call to mind again the fact that, while the itinerant storytellers, the *patuas*, have almost all disappeared today, their position has been taken over by the cinema in India. In both of these media colour, dance, song and many, many diversions are important elements, all part of the seduction of the audience. In this way the old tradition is transformed.

Part of an embroidered quilt, kantha. *This detail illustrating the parable of the Kingdom of the Rats presents an ironic comment on wealthy Bengalis: while they parade in European dress, the rats rule at home. Perhaps from Faridpur in modern Bangladesh, c.1870.*

The Future

Having looked in the preceding chapters at a number of stories from eastern India, what can we say about the future of mythic narrative in this region of the Indian subcontinent? Will it continue as a genre, entertaining and perhaps sometimes educating, or at least putting forward religious, political and social ideas, as it seems to have done since the first Buddhist missionaries travelled through eastern India in the late centuries BC? The answer may be that the progress of education and above all of literacy will determine the outcome. This is so because the stories described here are primarily ones that have descended to us through oral transmission. If the place and time available for storytelling in non-urban life disappear (the tradition has already largely vanished from urban life or been replaced by television), then the continuing development of narratives – existing ones and new ones – will cease. Those myths that have come down to us and have been recorded will remain, but the new ones will not be forthcoming or will be elaborated in a quite different way, probably through film or some electronic medium.

Some new stories have emerged over the last twenty-five years, and this gives grounds for confidence at least for the immediate future, although India is experiencing change today on a scale that was unimaginable even twenty-five years ago; what was true then is now out of date today. For this reason, it may be that even now we are witnessing the last gasp of this very ancient tradition in the handful of new narratives that have appeared in recent years.

One area for new stories has been in the arena of politics, especially in that uncomfortable region where politics and religion coincide. For instance, a good deal is known about the historical politician Mrs Indira Gandhi, but already her mythic existence is emerging as she herself disappears into history. Her life, with its developing mythic elements, has been depicted in scroll-paintings produced by an itinerant storyteller, Ajit Chitrakar, from Midnapore District, south-west of Calcutta. In this instance, the religious element is represented by the two Sikh bodyguards gunning down Mrs Gandhi in retaliation for the attack she had instigated on the Golden Temple in Amritsar; this episode has a prominent position in the scroll. Her life story is laid out in twelve registers, with a clear identification of her and India in the first register – she is shown rising out of the map of India as *Bharat-mata* (Mother India) – and in the final one she is being carried into heaven by Vishnu (see illustration overleaf). She has thus taken the first steps in the trajectory from the secular (ironically, always a rallying cry of her family) to the religious: she is becoming a goddess.

The existence of this painted scroll, and indeed of other examples illustrating more contemporary events such as the 2001 terrorist attack in New York

Indira Gandhi raised into heaven by Lord Vishnu following her assassination. Final panel in a storytelling scroll by the painter Ajit Chitrakar of Theakuachak, in the Midnapore District of West Bengal, mid-1980s.

or the 2005 tsunami, is reassuring in terms of storytelling survival. However, there is nevertheless the worry that the scroll was already aimed at a market far from the original one even when it was acquired by the present writer in 1986. It came from a demonstration at an art college by Ajit Chitrakar in a city (Baroda) far from Bengal, and has never been used. Finally, the painted scrolls produced today are in most instances made for the entertainment of a middle-class urban audience, rather than for the previous rural one. These scrolls represent the urban fascination with the hand-made and with the rural, while in the countryside such fascination works in reverse: there television, cinema and increasingly the internet are providing the narrative possibilities for today's population.

This change of purpose presents a fascinating and continuing paradox, but storytelling with scrolls is only a part of enjoying myths in Bengal. Happily, the puja celebrations continue to be an outlet for presenting the tales of the deities involved. The way in which, above all, the Durga Puja has reinvented itself during the whole of the twentieth century, moving from private, household devotion to public carnival and arts extravaganza (it must surely be the largest public arts festival anywhere in the world), is encouraging for the continuation of story transference. These changes are largely urban ones, but they are fuelled by the constant drawing in of new populations from the countryside, and this point of contact between city and countryside is probably the most important and most fertile activity for the development and re-emergence of narratives in Bengal. The future for myth-telling, indeed also for myth-making, in Bengal is perhaps not quite so bleak as it might otherwise appear, and in this context it is pertinent to remember what the greatest storyteller and poet of Bengal had to say on the subject of potentiality:

Deliverance is not for me in renunciation.
I feel the embrace of freedom in a thousand bonds of delight.
(Rabindranath Tagore, *Gitanjali*, London, 1913, no. 73)

Further Reading and Sources

For introductions to the culture of Bengal, see *Bengal: Sites and Sights*, ed. P. Pal and E. Haque (Mumbai, 2003); *The Arts of Bengal: The Heritage of Bangladesh and Eastern India*, ed. R. Skelton and M. Francis (London, 1979); and *Art and Life in Bangladesh* by H. Glassie (Indianapolis, 1997). For 18th-century culture, see the monumental *A Portrait of the Hindus: Balthazar Solvyns and the European Image of India 1760–1824* by R. Hardgrave (Oxford, 2004). Also very useful is the *Dictionary of Hindu Lore and Legend* by A. Dallapiccola (London, 2002), while Islam in Bengal is interestingly discussed in *The Islamic Syncretistic Tradition in Bengal* by A. Roy (Princeton, 1983) and *The Rise of Islam and the Bengal Frontier 1204–1760* by R. Eaton (Berkeley, 1993). For the architecture of Muslim Bengal, see *The Islamic Heritage of Bengal*, ed. G. Michell (Paris, 1984).

For investigation of the non-elite literature of Bengal, see D. Sen, *The Folk Literature of Bengal* (Calcutta, 1920), and E. Dimock, ed. and trans., *The Thief of Love: Bengal Tales from Court and Village* (Chicago, 1963), as well as *Fabulous Females and Peerless Pirs: Tales of Mad Adventure in Old Bengal*, trans. T.K. Stewart (Oxford, 2004). A quirky though useful study is *The Ritual Art of the Bratas of Bengal* by S.K. Ray (Calcutta, 1961). A recent study of Bengali literature can be found in 'The Two Histories of Literary Culture in Bengal' by S. Kaviraj in *Literary Cultures in History: Reconstructions from South Asia*, ed. S. Pollock (Berkeley, 2003).

For a helpful guide to Durga Puja in Calcutta today, see *Durga Puja: Yesterday, Today and Tomorrow*, by S. Banerjee (Delhi, 2004), while for the history of the Puja, see 'Durga Puja in Calcutta' by J. Chaliha and B. Gupta in *Calcutta: The Living City*, vol. II, ed. S. Chaudhuri (Calcutta, 1990). For the literature that surrounds devotion to both Durga and Kali, see *Mother of my Heart, Daughter of my Dreams: Kali and Uma in the Devotional Poetry of Bengal* by R.F. McDermott (Oxford, 2001) and, by the same author, *Singing to the Goddess: Poems to Kali and Uma from Bengal* (Oxford, 2001). For both Durga and Kali, see the relevant chapters in D. Kinsley's invaluable *Hindu Goddesses* (Delhi, 1987).

The literature on Krishna devotion in Bengal is large, but mention must be made of *The Place of the Hidden Moon* by E. Dimock (Chicago 1966). For Jayadeva, see *Love Song of the Dark Lord: Jayadeva's* Gitagovinda, ed. and trans. B.S. Miller (New York, 1977); for Chaitanya, see *The Chaitanya Movement* by M. Kennedy (Calcutta, 1925); and for Shankaradeva, see *Sankaradeva: Vaisnava Saint of Assam* by B. Barua (Gauhati, 1960). Meanwhile, for the architecture of Bengali Vaisnavism, note *Brick Temples of Bengal: From the Archives of David McCutchion*, ed. G. Michell (Princeton, 1983), and *Temple to Love* by P. Ghosh (Indianapolis, 2005). A useful book for the study of both Krishna and Kali is D. Kinsley's *The Sword and the Flute* (Berkeley, 1975).

On storytelling, see *Painting and Performance: Chinese Picture Recitation and its Indian Genesis* by V. Mair (Honolulu, 1988) and *Picture Showmen: Insights into the Narrative Tradition in Indian Art*, ed. J. Jain (Mumbai, 1998), including the article 'The "Murshidabad" Pats of Bengal' by T.R. Blurton. Also on Bengal storytelling, see Blurton's 'Continuity and change in the tradition of Bengali pata-painting', in *Shastric Traditions in Indian Arts*, ed. A. Dallapiccola (Stuttgart, 1989). A discussion of Bengali and other popular painting can be found in *From the Ocean of Painting: India's Popular Paintings 1589 to the Present* by B. Rossi (Oxford, 1998).

For the cult of Manasa, see *Historical Studies in the Cult of the Goddess Manasa* by P.K. Maity (Calcutta, 1966), and for Kamalekamini, see S. Nandi, 'A Scroll Painting on the Story of Kamalekamini … in the Indian Museum', *Indian Museum Bulletin* (Calcutta, 1970).

Picture Credits

Index